# IDEOLOGY AND EVERYDAY LIFE

ANTHROPOLOGY SERIES:
STUDIES IN CULTURAL ANALYSIS

Series Editor, Vern Carroll

# IDEOLOGY AND EVERYDAY LIFE

Anthropology, Neomarxist Thought, and
the Problem of Ideology and the Social Whole

*Steve Barnett*
*Martin G. Silverman*

THE UNIVERSITY OF MICHIGAN PRESS
ANN ARBOR

Published in the United States of America by
The University of Michigan Press and simultaneously
in Rexdale, Canada, by John Wiley & Sons Canada, Limited
Manufactured in the United States of America

**Library of Congress Cataloging in Publication Data**

Barnett, Steve, 1941-
   Ideology and everyday life.

   (Anthropology series: Studies in cultural analysis)
   Includes bibliographical references.
   1. Ethnology. 2. Communism and anthropology.
I. Silverman, Martin G., joint author. II. Title.
III. Series.
GN345.B27   301.2   79-14545
ISBN 0-472-02704-2

# CONTENTS

# PREFACE AND ACKNOWLEDGMENTS

In anthropology and related fields today we encounter the realization that while many basic issues have been clarified in the past century, many basic issues have also been obscured. And as part of this realization people are turning increasingly to the works of founding figures such as Marx, Maine, Weber, Simmel, Durkheim and Mauss (cf. Becker 1971). We are reading these people both as actors in a history of which we are part, and as sources of insights which have been explored insufficiently in the period intervening between their times and our own.

In their times, significant shifts in the organization of production were taking place, and in our time significant shifts in the organization of production are taking place. Perhaps such shifts incline us to wonder about the foundations of our knowledge and about the relation between that knowledge and the processes which pertain to its construction. As far as anthropology is concerned, we feel that this questioning becomes most interesting when it involves concrete problems in the conduct of ethnography and the organization of ethnographic data and ethnographic understanding.

Within anthropological theory there are currently a number of comprehensive and productive challenges to existing modes of analysis, challenges which recognize the importance of the connections between theory and ethnography, and the connections between ethnography, theory and the larger world in which they are practiced. These challenges can be very loosely grouped under the headings of neomarxist and critical analyses; symbolic, structuralist and communicational analyses; and feminist analyses.

We hope that the chapters in this volume will be seen in the context of, and as a contribution to, attempts to deal with some of the issues raised by these challenges. Both of us have been worrying about these things for some time. Many colleagues and students have worried about them with us. To them we make a necessarily abstract acknowledgment.

The first two chapters were written by both of us and represent attempts to deal with theories and findings from the sources mentioned. The third chapter is not a joint effort in the same sense, but we found that as a draft of one chapter was (apparently) completed, certain things in the drafts of the other chapters had to be changed. Colleagues who read earlier versions of the chapters will thus find additions, deletions and shifts. The development of the volume has been a dialectical one.

The third chapter is partially a reworking of material previously presented elsewhere (e.g., Silverman 1971, 1972), and partially an attempt to relate that material to what we know about other Oceanic societies. Silverman found that his previous presentations left too many theoretical loose ends, and those presentations were difficult to integrate with the available ethnography on Gilbertese-speaking and related peoples. The present construction is, among other things, a product of trying to deal with those loose ends, of trying to embed the ethnography in older and newer knowledge of the region (see especially Labby 1976a, 1976b), and of our joint efforts. The present construction of the ethnography, as well as Silverman's own contributions to the first two chapters, is also a consequence of working in the Canadian academic environment, in which there is a very important critical anthropological and sociological component.

Throughout this work our emphasis is on the concrete analysis of specific ideological forms, either Euro-North American or Banaban and Gilbertese. We hope the reader will focus on these concrete points, hence we have not discussed certain crucial issues in anthropological history or marxist discourse that would simply occupy too many pages and which would blunt our main points. For example, we obviously use concepts and orientations given in Durkheim's *Division of Labor in Society* (Durkheim 1933 [1902]) and in Lukács' *History and Class Consciousness* (Lukács 1971), yet we only allude to these authors. Similarly, we raise the question of the nature of totality and reification, but do not discuss them as such in sufficient detail, preferring to let our points emerge from the analysis of specific ideological forms. This is intentional; we want readers to focus on ideology in the advanced monopoly capitalism of Euro-North America, and on the question of how one can deal with the discussion of "ideological" matters in the holistic reconstruction of a radically different social collectivity. We plan further books and papers discussing precisely the etiology of these complex and important concepts and beg the knowledgeable reader's indulgence for our present approach.

Silverman expresses his appreciation to the Social Science Research Council (U.S.A.) for a Grant in Method and Theory

(1973-1974); and to the Department of Pacific and Southeast Asian History, Australian National University, for a Visiting Fellowship (1973-1974), under the joint tenure of which he developed some of the material included in this volume. The later Professor J. W. Davidson, and Dr. D. Scarr, were very helpful in Canberra. The research was also made possible by a leave of absence from the University of Western Ontario, and by research grants from that university's Dean of the Faculty of Social Sciences.

For editorial help we would like to thank Ms. R. Silverman and Professor V. Carroll.

For typing, we would like to thank Ms. R. Walsh, Ms. A. Donovan-Graham, Ms. Z. Sabur, Ms. D. Green, Ms. M. Garroway and Ms. E. Jamal.

We express our appreciation to publishers, authors or editors for permission to quote from the following sources:

W. H. Geddes, *North Tabiteuea Report* (Victoria University of Wellington, Rural Socio-Economic Survey of the Gilbert and Ellice Islands; Wellington: Victoria University of Wellington, 1975), by permission of the author and with the kind permission of the Minister of Local Government, Gilbert Islands; Arthur Grimble, "From birth to death in the Gilbert Islands," *Journal of the Royal Anthropological Institute* 51(1921):25-54, by permission of the Royal Anthropological Institute of Great Britain and Ireland; Bernd Lambert, "Rank and Ramage in the Northern Gilbert Islands" (Ph.D. dissertation, University of California, Berkeley, 1963), by permission of the author; David Schneider, "Kinship, nationality and religion in American culture: toward a definition of kinship," in Robert F. Spencer, ed., *Forms of Symbolic Action*, pp. 116-125 (Proceedings of the 1969 Annual Spring Meeting, American Ethnological Society, 1970), by permission of the author and the editor; Marilyn Strathern, "The achievement of sex: Paradoxes in Hagen gender-thinking" (manuscript, to be published in the *Yearbook of Symbolic Anthropology*), by permission of the author.

# IMPASSES IN SOCIAL THEORY

It is the thesis of our volume that this moment in the development of Western anthropological theory is characterized by two impasses: an impasse within the general range of liberal anthropological (and related) theory, and an impasse within the general range of neomarxist (and related) theory. In both we are encountering difficulties, dilemmas and contradictions which have to do with the nature of ideology and with the nature of the social whole, the latter issue encompassing the former.[1]

We further propose that these dilemmas are very closely related to dilemmas in social action.

We feel that results from both the liberal and neomarxist traditions can be utilized by posing, as a central analytic issue, the issue of the basic separations which people make in their life activity. This volume will attempt to explicate, in a very preliminary way, how one can think in terms of such basic separations.

By using this deceptively simple phrase ("the basic separations which people make in their life activity"), we do not mean to invoke, for example, the present anthropological approach of cognitive anthropology, in which one studies systems of classification, of categories, perhaps suggesting that each society or sub-group divides up the pie of reality a little differently. Rather, we take the idea of separations to direct our attention toward fundamentally different approaches to categorization itself, toward what is prior to the understanding and existence of any concrete category. Raising this issue moves one to inquire into how people construct the relation of the self to the social whole, which in turn moves us toward relations of production.

Rather than seeing separations as a given fact in the world, and therefore ending up with something like the universal continua of Parsons' pattern variables (Parsons 1951), or a universal etic grid (Tyler 1969), we are working toward a theory of separations. Foucault's *The Order of Things* (Foucault 1973 [1966]) is perhaps the clearest recent indication that such a theory is necessary,

* In chapters 1 and 2, where we feel it necessary to indicate that we are referring to the use of a term or concept as part of everyday discourse, we set it off in single quotes; where we feel it necessary to indicate that we are referring to the use of a term or concept as part of social science or marxist discourse, we set it off in double quotes. In chapter 3, single quotes are used for glosses of Banaban and Gilbertese words, concepts and conventional phrases.

and we can also point to questions raised by Bateson (e.g., Bateson 1972). [2]

In Chapter 2, we discuss the internal connections among the representations of persons, things, units and relations which are part of the unity of determinations of many Western capitalist societies. Through understanding the separations which are presupposed, we can understand many of the dilemmas and taken-for-granted aspects of everyday life in capitalist societies generally, and in anthropology specifically.

In Chapter 3, we try to show how some of the same sorts of questions raised in Chapter 2 can illuminate the understanding of gender relations in precolonial Banaban and Gilbertese societies (Central Pacific).

Here the points in Chapter 3 join the points in Chapter 2. For these two very different social formations (capitalist and non-capitalist), we try to demonstrate that in order to understand the relations between the basic separations which people make, one must embed those basic separations in the different "relations of production" of the different societies. At the same time, the very construction of the concept of relations of production must respond to the facts of the particular case.

Trying to utilize neomarxist approaches in Oceania is particularly attractive, since many of the Oceanic peoples have themselves elaborated activities and meanings having to do with production, reproduction, productivity, growth. [3] At least for many of these peoples, we feel it is possible to take neomarxist orientations and illuminate, rather than obscure, the internal relations among their practices.

By saying "internal relations" (following Ollman 1971, and drawing on Althusser 1969, and Althusser and Balibar 1970), we are trying to take very seriously an anthropological homily, but a homily which can be overlooked with the development of systems theory and cybernetic approaches (see below). The things we are talking about are already interrelated as part of a complex totality, in which their existences-definitions are contingent upon one another. Their "interrelations" are more like the interrelations between the two sides of a page than they are like the interrelations between "variables" such as rainfall and garden productivity.

In the current chapter, we provide a brief discussion of the grounding for the kinds of questions raised in Chapters 2 and 3. These questions follow from our sense of the dilemmas many social scientists are in, and from our interpretations of the societies under discussion.

## FROM THE SIDE OF LIBERAL ANTHROPOLOGICAL (AND RELATED) THEORY

*Sameness and Difference, Universality and Particularity.* Anthropology as a theoretical enterprise is constituted by the contradiction between sameness and difference. Stated otherwise, we find in anthropology notions of both the universality of something (culture, roles, minds, biology, the human condition, whatever) and the particularity of specific instances (this culture versus that culture, and so forth). At different moments and in different circles in the history of anthropology, one or the other is stressed: the samenesses, universalities and naturalnesses; the differences, particularities and arbitrarinesses.

Noting the importance of this contradiction gives one pause when one realizes that it is not far from a certain Western common sense apprehension: on the one hand, "human nature is the same everywhere;" on the other hand, "everyone is different; how can you generalize?"

By presenting the structures of other societies as fundamentally variations on the same themes which govern our own, we are able to empathize and to sympathize with other peoples. At the same time, we can imagine that we discover that our own form of society is but a particle of the universal human condition. Our own form of society can become justified in the process. The issue might not be a real one were it not for the fact that the actions of people in the societies which most anthropologists come from can have a much more powerful impact on the actions of people in the societies studied than vice-versa.

An extreme alternative is presenting other peoples in terms which are radically different from the terms in which we understand ourselves. Then those other peoples might seem almost to be people from another galaxy, and hence alien, difficult to empathize with, difficult to sympathize with. Therefore their exploitation would present less of an intellectual problem for us, and we might care even less about them, and about the implications of our own actions for them and vice-versa.

If the particularity and difference aspect of the contradiction is abolished, it becomes possible for dominated peoples to make claims on dominating people of the same order as different segments of the dominating group make on each other. But on the same basis, the dominating group can refuse such claims on the ground that acceding to them would be 'less efficient' than acceding to others.

If the universality and sameness aspect of the contradiction is abolished, it becomes possible for dominated peoples to assert vigorously that they have been manipulated by alien intruders. But on the same basis, the dominating can reply: if we are so alien to one another, how can we even 'negotiate', what is the basis of that 'obligation' which binds us to them so that we must treat them as equally human and as 'deserving'?

If the particularity and difference aspect of the contradiction is abolished, social science justifies itself as the study of The Human Condition. With the assumption of genuine sameness, the possibility of understanding increases. But then why after so much study should one go all the way to other places to find out what the Human Condition is about? Why study history?

If the universality and sameness aspect of the contradiction is abolished, the study of any one people by 'qualified' representatives of another people becomes as justified as is the study of anything else. But then we raise doubts about the possibility of understanding others, and why bother, anyway, unless we have a concrete interest in governing them or in trading with them?

These contradictions can double-bind us all, and are double-binding many of us.[4] They are not universal, and in order to understand why we should be caught in them we must understand something beyond anthropology itself.

In addition to the general apprehension of both sameness and difference, many anthropological approaches share another characteristic with Western assumptions: that a language of description and analysis exists which can make sense out of other peoples' social formations through using the same terms as one uses for one's own.[5]

Thus we 'have families' and they have families; their families just happen to be of a different kind than ours (e.g., extended as opposed to nuclear). This is the sort of characterization which seems to allow for the simultaneous expression of both sameness and difference, of both universality and particularity. A system characterized by nuclear families is different from a system characterized by extended families, yet both systems can be characterized as systems involving families. The logic is similar to that which identifies political struggles in terms of, say, Right and Left political opinions. Right and Left opinions are different from one another, indeed contrast with one another, yet both are equally political opinions, perhaps both are regarded as being equally legitimate.

As for families, so too for other concepts: religion, economic system, language, law. Immediately as one poses a question of the following form: how does their kinship system differ from our kinship system?, one is assuming some notion of kinship system applicable to them and to us, or one creates the problem of finding shared characteristics. If one takes the position (see below) that there is not such a unity, then other and equally serious dilemmas arise.

While we may state as part of an anthropological homily that a concept such as kinship system is an abstraction, given that the concept is close to our own common sense categories, we can point to certain things which we 'know' to be 'real' which fit those abstractions. After all, most of us can identify our own families, or can identify a particular church as having to do with religion.

*Stances Toward Analytic Categories.* The denial of the existence of categories such as kinship, religion, economy, etc., in our own culture would be absurd. Equally absurd would be the denial that we are in our own work influenced by the existence of such categories. But there are *(inter alia)* two ways of incorporating such categories into anthropological research.[6]

(1) In one usage, these categories are what we may call "categories of convenience." The object of research is not to fill in a number of blanks under the category label, but to transcend the categories to uncover the unities which exist internally in a particular culture. If, for example, by asking questions about kinship we learn that in another culture much of what appears as kinship to us, has to do with the relations between people and land,

kinship disappears as a relevant analytic category, and is replaced by "the relations between people and land." If in that culture in order to discuss the relations between people and land one has to discuss the concepts, forms and uses of agricultural implements, that is simply what one has to do. One might not have to do that in an analysis which begins with kinship, in another place.

As one does this, however, one has opened the door to a much larger issue, especially if a comparative objective remains: in order to understand why certain things go together in one place one must also understand how those things are differentiated from things which do not go together with them. The categories of convenience point of departure leads to a consideration not of fragments, but of social wholes. The study of kinship among the X leads to a broader study of the X.

(2) In another usage, these categories are taken as the terms of a general social theory, or at least as the terms for the organization of data, the organization of university courses, monograph chapters, textbooks and articles (the economy of the X, the relation between C and D among the Y). Since these categories are taken seriously, one can generate an infinity of questions for research, writing and teaching: questions phrased relationally, comparatively, historically, even in an evolutionary system. The strongest use of such categories is in the identification of sub-systems: the religious sub-system, the economic sub-system, the legal sub-system, and so forth. Having identified sub-systems, to be elegant one must construct some notion of the glue which binds them together (e.g., generalized values), or perhaps indicate how they are in conflict (negative glue, if you will).

Some inkling of difficulty here may be gleaned from the fact that in a number of societies, it is difficult to point to particular groups of institutions and identify them as kinship institutions as distinct from, say, economic institutions. By definition such societies may be considered less complex, and the language used to describe the situation is that kinship and economy are not "strongly differentiated" or that economic transactions are "embedded" in kinship relations. Or, at the boundary between liberal and neomarxist traditions, it may be asserted that kinship relations function both as infrastructure and as superstructure.[7] The point of reference here is, of course, 'our own system' (or rather the ideology of it; see below), in which things are more highly differentiated, less embedded, or more clearly divided into infrastructure and superstructure. (This is reminiscent of other origin myths which take up the theme: the formation of The Many out of The One.)

A set of conceptual problems is created by the apprehension that certain distinctions have more utility in one situation than in another situation. There are a variety of moves which seem to permit the identification of differences, but the categories are still not questioned in their very essence.

The difficulty with these categories (e.g., kinship, religion, politics, law) which has been the subject of some recent discussion can be formulated as follows: do the instances of a category in different cultures share any structurally significant characteristic other than the fact that we choose to regard them as instances of the same category?[8]

For example, accepting these terms for the moment: if in one setting, "political activities" occur in the context of parties, and in another setting political activities occur in the context of kinship relations, what do we achieve by using the notion of political activities? Why not just talk about parties and their relations to other elements in the first case, and kinship and its relations to other elements in the second? What do we achieve other than our own peace of mind, a tenuous validation of notions of universality, and a justification of our specialties, departments, courses, and so forth?

What we seem to achieve, of course, is a way to compare different societies and cultures, or rather, to compare "analytically distinguishable aspects" of different societies and cultures. Without such concepts, comparison appears impossible; the comparison of analytically distinguishable aspects, abstracted from the social whole of which they are part, appears impossible.

There is a sort of compromise move here, in which one maintains the use of such categories (kinship, economy, religion, etc.), but specifies the variation in terms of the "dominance" of one versus the other. This is a move which one, again, finds at the boundary between liberal and neomarxist anthropology.[9] Immediately, however, this move runs into the Structuralist's Dilemma: if kinship is dominant over politics in situation X, and politics is dominant over kinship in situation Y, are the kinship and the politics in both cases really the same sort of thing? Or, is this a shorthand for talking about something more complex? The apprehended difficulties in the utility of the concepts seem to be resolved by making the concepts' referents more or less dominant over one another. But the structuralist's dilemma remains. Either one has to say that the concepts are being used as a sort of short-hand, in which case one is back into the first usage (categories of convenience, and the problems which derive from it), or one is saying that they do have some precise meaning which is universal, in which case one is asserting a sort of universal repertoire of un-situated, ahistorical elements, which combine here and there with more or less force, which are then reified to the point of obscur-ing rather than illuminating the relations between people and their life activities.

*Analytic Categories and Wholes.* The option of rejecting com-parison altogether is unacceptable unless one imagines an anthro-pology conducted by people in their own culture, more or less ignorant of other cultures. This is so because, generally speaking, all anthropology conducted by members of one society in an-other is at least implicitly comparative, the point of comparison being the investigators' understandings of their own culture.

Therefore, unless one arbitrarily posits a world of ahistorical definitions (or elements), and blinds oneself to all the difficul-ties in the transcultural use of categories of this sort, the issue of the social whole appears here also. What is required is a theory of the whole, or theories of wholes.

However, the earlier problems reproduce themselves at this level: if one needs a theory of the whole (or theories of wholes), what are the terms of analysis which would be part of such a theory? Is the question of the nature of the scope of a specific whole a question with a presupposed answer, or an answer to be discovered?

We might illuminate many of the dilemmas by taking a second look at some of the concepts which have been used to deal with analytic pieces, often with the presupposition that they link up into a unified theory of all wholes: the use for comparative pur-poses of notions such as kinship, religion, economy.

One sort of criticism is by now well-worn: we must be careful not to assume that something we have in our own form of society (e.g., nuclear families, monotheistic religions, centralized political systems) is found in all other societies. The stronger version of this critique is the point raised earlier: that instances of the more general categories (kinship, religion, politics) may share nothing of structural significance other than the fact that we agglomerate them under the same label, and then create for ourselves the manifold problems of how they are similar and different from one another, and how they relate to one another.

There is, however, another aspect of the critique which must be dredged up. Critical analysts often assume that these terms identify something more or less unproblematically real (as units) or analytically useful in our own form of society. To what extent is this assumption warranted? Or: if these terms mystify the internal ordering of other social forms, might they not also mystify the internal ordering of our own social forms?

Consider, for example, the family. Let us accept for the moment D. M. Schneider's (1968) proposition that for the white, urban American middle class, the paradigmatic family is a unit of parents and children living together: the co-resident nuclear family. This is a folk definition of the family. Let us also assume for the purposes of argument that most units identified as being really families correspond to this definition (assuming otherwise would make our argument even easier). Let us further assume that people regard families as operating in roughly similar ways.

Now, as we inspect these units as they are "on the ground," we find that there are families where all adult members 'work' and there are families where no adult members 'work'. There are families, the members of which produce a good deal of what they consume; there are families the members of which produce very little of what they consume. There are families in which everyone shares the housework, there are families in which only one adult woman is involved in housework. In each of these cases, if one thinks out the implications, 'the family' articulates in different ways with institutions which even the natives think of as being 'outside' the family.

If our analyses of Western societies presuppose that these families are units of the same order, then these analyses can be criticized in the same manner as studies which assert that in all cultures there are families which are, essentially, of the same sort. The analyst within Western society is either accepting the natives' own definition of 'the family', or is in effect asserting that those characteristics that analytically grasp what is most important about what is going on just happen to correspond to the natives' definition. (The same point can be made about things happening 'inside' the family, if we accept notions such as "socialization" and "personality." If there are families in which the members love and support one another, and families in which the members repress one another, these are conceivable as different ways in which socialization is carried out!)

If we are looking for the structures and functions of family units in this form of society, and if we determine that the only thing of significance shared by these units is that the natives (the members of the units, and the members of government agencies and other instrumentalities which deal with them as 'families') deem them to be families—and, furthermore, similar families—we are faced with an interesting analytic question: in spite of monumental structural and functional differences, these people term all these units 'families', and operate with the assumption that a variety of other things go along with the existence of such units. The analytic question is: why? The same point may be made about curtains, pieces of chalk and fish, but to both natives and their analysts, the category 'family' occupies a rather different position than do the categories curtains, pieces of chalk and fish.

The issue is, of course, clearest for the concept 'economy'. Something is surely being missed if what the owners of IBM can do and do do in their 'business', and what the owners of a small market garden can do and do do in their 'business', are both seen as just "different forms of economic action."

One really begins to suspect that many standard categories (e.g., 'family') are inadequate not only for the description of "other societies" but also for the description of "our own," when people argue about the "political" functions of "economic units" (e.g., multinational corporations), or about the "economic" functions of "political units" (e.g., the State). Worries about the usefulness of social science categories are not new, but may take a particular shape under the current conditions of monopoly capitalism.

Categories such as kinship, economic, political, property, are categories of our own ideology, and can reveal certain relations among phenomena in Western societies. But such categories can also distort certain relations by posing boundaries between elements which are internally linked (e.g., separating the analysis of imperialism from the analysis of the free market), and by combining elements of different orders (e.g., "property" as the ownership of a pencil and of a corporation producing pencils). In the next chapter we do not make the notions of certain units (e.g. the family) problematic enough ourselves, but try to cover some of the ground which is necessary as a preliminary to a more comprehensive critical analysis.

*The Problem of a Domain of Ideological Content.* Much of our repertoire of analytic categories can be seen not as concepts designed for the analytic description of what surrounds us, but as concepts which are themselves part of that process which is the reproduction of our own social form. Recall Lévi-Strauss' dictum (1963) that people's conscious models exist to perpetuate, not to explain, social phenomena. While one may question the point as a universal point, one can accept it in the present case.

In order to entertain such possibilities, however, one must be able to speak of ideology, and ideology as it is itself an aspect of something larger. That is, one must already have an inkling of the whole. There is no way out of this problem. In order to deal critically with our categories of analysis, we must have an analysis of them: an analysis which, if it does not relate them to a world larger than those categories, can be accused of merely participating in the reproduction of this social form.

L. Dumont's work is perhaps the most significant recent attempt to construct comparison on a large scale (Dumont 1961, 1970), a comparison which does not abolish the differences between the peoples concerned. His conception actually turns on those differences, and on the implications of being internal to one form of society and studying another. Dumont emphasizes the contrasts in stressed aspects of "ideology" between India and the West. But there is another problem here: to the extent that Dumont's basic contrast, individualism/holism, has the form of a Parsonian pattern variable, it reifies the category of ideology and places us in a universe of eternal oscillation between poles which then have the appearance of being simply given in the human condition. We find here the recreation of the original problem, but on a much higher level: if we are to construct our analysis of the whole through stressed aspects of ideology, then, in effect, we cannot make problematic the relation between ideology and other aspects of the whole. We are back in the same bind as that in which politics and economy may be seen as more or less dominant in different social formations. The conceptual apparatus we use must enable us to ask questions about the relation between ideology and "other things," but to the point of enabling us to question the utility of the category ideology itself. Otherwise, one is in the indefensible because dogmatic position of declaring some categories to be susceptible to critical analysis, while other categories are somehow immune. Thus, at the outset, the last thing we would want to do would be to give a definition of ideology as a subject matter. To say in any other than a loose way, "by ideology we mean. . .," would meet certain analysts' requirements for scholarly discourse, but would reproduce in this work the dilemmas which we are interested in talking about. Such a definition if made at the beginning of analysis would be liable to the same sort of critique made of the notion of family. It is true enough that in any analysis one must assume something, but in this analysis we need not assume a cross-culturally uniform domain of ideology. Definitions which might seem acceptable are vague, and rightly so.

There are a number of signs of a shift of attention away from the attempt to prescribe definitions of ideology, culture, symbol and related constructs, and toward the attempt to delineate the conditions under which such domains are posited, and institutionalized in academic and other settings. [10]

*The Problem of Ideological Form.* Where the problem of ideology obtrudes, within the Western anthropological tradition, attempts to solve our dilemmas with comparative categories seem to recreate the dilemmas they are oriented to solving. We might not, in fact, be capable of transcending such difficulties entirely. But at least we can attempt to gain a clearer insight into these dilemmas by turning to the links between ideology and that to which ideology is related, sustaining the notion that such links are not everywhere of the same kind.

This is, of course, not a novel proposition. Using "cultural system" and "social system" language, Parsons in his evolutionary approach writes of the relative degree of "differentiation" between such systems (Parsons 1966; see also Bellah 1964). Thus the relationship between these "analytically separable" systems is at this analytic level not a constant; the possibility of systematic variation is acknowledged. This is, in its own way, a step forward, considered vis-à-vis a position that social structures simply emanate from cultural structures, or vice-versa, or that there is a dialectical relation between the two. For the conception here (perhaps one might call it the Weber-Parsons-Bellah conception) allows us to think about the relationship of ideological form to that with which ideological form is related. For example, the notion of the "rationalization of the symbolic system" is a notion qualitatively different from the notion of a "value on achievement" or "an emphasis on ancestor worship." Similarly, Lévi-Strauss' distinction between bricolage and science raises questions of ideological form. The works of Whorf and D. Lee do also. [11]

As the next chapter should make clear, we feel that the work within anthropology which is most useful for the illumination of our dilemmas comes not so much from the self-declared materialists, as from the approaches which are, explicitly or implicitly, more toward the idealist end. This is so because the latter approaches have pursued the issue of how various ideological constructions articulate with one another, and it is through an understanding of those modes of articulation that the links to other things are to be discerned.

Turning to anthropology itself, a critical analysis which would pose the theoretical dilemma as, say, the contrast and conflict between idealist and materialist approaches is an analysis which stops short of the point. The point is, rather, how it is possible for such a contrast to be drawn as a contrast, how such a contrast is used (in research, teaching, situations of theoretical and other struggle), how the contrast and conflict articulate with the practice of anthropology in relation to the social whole of which this practice is part.

Let us imagine for a moment how we could begin to look at ideological form in anthropology. Anthropology is very largely a "vocation of opinion" in Sartre's sense (Sartre 1965: 73-74), and there must be a clientele attracted (or delivered) to an anthropologist's (or approach's) reputation. Where one of the means

toward gaining reputation is giving the appearance of a certain
degree of intellectual novelty—but within an acceptable range—we
might well expect theoretical and methodological development to
occur through structural reversals and mediations. Emphases on
the individual vs. emphases on society; emphases on biology vs.
emphases on culture; emphases on intuitive apprehension vs. emphases on empiricist hardware, and so forth. As anthropology is
periodically concerned with differentiating itself from other
disciplines (other disciplines, being older, better placed, or both,
do not appear so concerned with differentiating themselves from
anthropology), anthropologies are concerned with differentiating
themselves from other anthropologies, anthropologists are concerned with differentiating themselves from other anthropologists. This is the logic of product differentiation, and the point is
not merely analogic. Departments of anthropology literally advertise for a marxist anthropologist (rarely!), a symbolic anthropologist, a political anthropologist. Would-be appointees literally
advertise themselves in these terms. Books and monographs are
literally advertised using these categories. What might in one
sense be regarded as analytic categories and distinctions (marxist, symbolic, political, etc.) have become real as part of the practice of anthropology. How are we to think of this?

In some quarters, the heritage of the flowering of jobs and
approaches in the 1950's (see Murphy 1971) seems to be a certain methodological relativism which may be a transformation of
cultural relativism, which is itself a transformation of pluralism.
Every theory, like every culture, like every 'ethnic group', has its
own and equal authenticity.

Of course it is never really "every theory," as it was never
really "every" culture and every ethnic group or ideology. And
the naively pluralistic point of view is one which (1) generously
puts others on the same uncertain footing as oneself, while (2)
denying to others the legitimacy of demonstrating their greater
validity. And a fractionation occurs. For example: the useful
bit in structuralism allows us to understand the logic of mythology. The useful bit in functionalism allows us to understand
the relation of ritual to ecology. The useful bit in componential
analysis allows us to understand plant categories. The useful bit
in marxism allows us to understand the necessity of imperialist

expansion. When we cannot fit things together, we can always call them different sub-systems.

While each method may make its own claim to generality, one seems to have the options, especially in teaching, of (1) dogmatism in favor of one claim to generality, (2) treating the theoretical variability in terms of its historical development (thus anthropological theory becomes the history of itself, but this runs up against the dilemma of how to conceptualize that history), (3) playing a number of different approaches against "the same data" (or almost the same data; the relations between different theories and their relations to data then approximate the relations between symphonic and Muzak renderings of 'the same song'), or (4) eclectically drawing from a fraction of one method which seems to handle a fraction of reality successfully, and a fraction of another method which seems to handle another fraction of reality successfully. As the problem is sensed, the demand for more comprehensive theory and methods increases (the universalizing side), while at the same time theories and methods contract to the cubbyholes of reality or illusion (the particularizing side), where rigor can become rigor mortis. [12]

From at least the pedagogical point of view, there is a real danger. The differences upon which we center our discussion begin to refer to other theories, methods and anthropologists, rather than to (non-anthropologist) peoples. The correct requirement that one situate an analysis theoretically can tend to make an analysis the illustration of one approach in contrast to other approaches, much as a particular piece of furniture is fashioned as an example of Motel Modern rather than Plastic Mediterranean. The issue passes into the issue not of the relations (logical or real) of peoples to one another, but of the relations of anthropologies or anthropologists to one another: the issue, say, of the relation between structuralism and functionalism, or marxism, or cybernetics, as often as not reduced to examination slogans except in the most theoretically skilled hands.

The world now appears as a world of anthropological theory and theorists, with important positions in the tradition and politics of the discipline. The similarities and differences between the theorists (or theories) become primary. The referent of structuralism is no longer Bororo villages, say, or even the Bororo people.

The referent is functionalism, marxism, and so forth, or Lévi-Strauss vs. Needham vs. Schneider vs. Fortes vs. Dumont. The final move is in a way the discounting maneuver which one occasionally hears: "Oh well, that's a functionalist interpretation," or a "marxist interpretation," or an "alliance theory interpretation," thus solving the problems of understanding!

Theory succumbs to the logic of fashion, as these differences (like ascot vs. necktie) refer mainly to one another, as Barthes might put it. This is decadence, often under the guise of self-reflection, as when rock singers sing rock songs about rock singers singing rock songs, unto the golden gates of Rock and Roll Heaven. The meta-metaphor, in a way, is to see culture (or social action) as metaphor, or as text: the world as seminar, the world as the pages of the *American Anthropologist*. [13] One does not have to be a deeply committed marxist or materialist to be more than a little suspicious of such views of what human behavior is all about, when, miraculously, Everyman and Everywoman are going about doing essentially what anthropologists go about doing, except that anthropologists do it for a living!

The understanding of anthropology and the understanding of the social whole of which it is part inform one another. We take the fashion metaphor not merely as a metaphor, but as pointing to underlying similarities between the ways in which the nature of anthropological theories, political opinions, fashions, ethnic groups or cultures are posed in liberal advanced monopoly capitalist society. [14] Differences are constructed which refer to other differences in a universe of potentially substitutable products. But the structure of the relations between these potentially substitutable products is not arbitrary. There are, after all, certain very definite "social relations" which determine whether the one open departmental position will be advertised for a symbolic anthropologist or for a cultural ecologist, and there are certain very definite social relations which determine who will get the job, and who will not.

FROM THE SIDE OF NEOMARXISM: THINKING CAPITAL

*Domains and Convergence.* We can say that the anthropological problem is how to move across space without merely carrying our own cultural baggage with us. Carrying this baggage creates a barrier to our appreciation of any other social formation, as well as to our appreception of our own social formation. The neomarxist problem is how to move across time without carrying that baggage, and of course not merely to move across time, but, for some, to participate in social transformation.

What we learn from the anthropological impasse is this. Given no concept of a social whole, there is no basis for isolating comparable analytic domains across cultures. The marxist impasse has a similar form. While Marx himself did nothing if not attempt to create a theory of a social whole, the depiction of that whole in certain branches of neomarxist theory appears increasingly based on a rigid formulation and separation of domains such as base, infrastructure and superstructure, as a substitution for a theory of social wholes.

The neomarxist impasse has a particular subtlety, which is also a particular tragedy. This is because neomarxist categories (if studied in their historical genesis) are intended to criticize the appearance of ideological representations as if they are realities which are given in the world. Neomarxist categories are supposed to methodologically (at least) strip us of the ideological baggage which reproduces our particular social formation. To the extent that these categories become appropriated within liberal discourse, their use has an effect which is exactly opposite to what Marx intended. Yet this has occurred. Given our understanding of domains as at least partially autonomous, for "base," "infrastructure," "superstructure," one can read "economic system," "social system," cultural system." Add "personality system," assume an often ad hoc causality that starts with "economics," and the appropriation is complete. [15]

Some marxists see this apparent convergence (paralleling arguments about the convergence of the U.S. and the U.S.S.R. as "social systems") as positive, and develop a systems theory and cybernetic vocabulary. A burgeoning literature is developing along these lines, and dialogues are encouraged. All that is lacking from this convergence is significant activity to ameliorate the present alienation and oppression of those not participating in such dialogues.

Raising the question of the convergence of aspects of marxist

and non-marxist social theory raises the question of the nature of
the social whole and its putative component units. Just as within
anthropology, when these units are regarded as existing as units in
themselves, the posing of subsequent problems presupposes that
the question of the social whole and its constituents is a settled
matter. From a marxist perspective, the matter can never be
settled. To the extent to which such units can be made to express
the reproduction of advanced monopoly capitalism, they are reifications, and convergence of of capitalist and socialist thought is
thus one-sided. But it is easier to suggest starting at each point
with the social whole than to take it as a practical task.

It is thus no accident that marxists concerned with understanding and isolating ideology as form can be atrracted to the two
most profound recent developments of liberal social thought:
systems theory and structuralism. Each offers a model primarily
for filling in and completing the form of a domain, and only sec-
ondarily for linking domains. Systems theory can generate sub-
systems, the connections of which can require unusually severe
acts of faith to sustain. Some varieties of structuralism provide
sets of binary opposites, but either cannot order these opposites
in terms of their primacy within a structure, or when engaging
in such an ordering, recreate the Structuralist's Dilemma (discussed in the previous section).[16]

Neither structuralism nor systems theory provides a self-reflexive understanding of the act of domain creation itself. Neither
has taken us to the meta-level of asking what a domain (or a category, a boundary, a distinction) is. It will not do to appeal to a
general cultural tendency, or to an innate human tendency, which
impels people to construct categories and to draw distinctions.
That sort of universalism acts to deflect attention away from the
meta-level, rather than to force attention to it, and, of course, can
make no real sense of the words *innate, human* or *tendency*.

The point of this volume of exploratory essays can be summarized as an attempt to think about our construction of and our
living within domains and boundaries, as an aspect of our ideology, as our problematic, not as a reflection of the way things
are.[17] And this suggests how one might think about the posing
of scientific vs. ideological questions about human society. A
scientific question is posed so that the social whole, not a prior

abstract category, is the immediate analytic referent. An ideological question starts with a necessarily reified domain or sub-system.

*Setting Up the Problem Through Marx. Capital,* in a sense creating the outlines for future marxist analyses, itself posed a difficult problem for those who wrote later. Given the needs of the socialist movement of the time, and given Marx's necessary preoccupation with finding an objective footing for a labor theory of value (as social relation, not subjective "need"), the focus of *Capital* was a critique of political economy. Marx performed the initial cuts into the social whole by attacking the categories of bourgeois political economy. Unlike Marx, those following him had available to them both the idea of a social whole and a set of already given analytic distinctions, such as base, infrastructure and superstructure. But those distinctions were not systematically linked throughout *Capital;* the precise formulation of that linkage was not part of the project of the moment, as Engels later lamented. [18]

Marxists find certain divisions already given and endow their form with analytic priority as one way of returning to the understanding of the nature of the whole. But as the nature of the divisions becomes the most important question, the nature of the whole becomes the least important question. After Marx, it was possible to argue that he really did provide a theory that either neatly grounded the superstructure in the base, or allowed the superstructure's relative autonomy. It was "easier" (i.e., one could get on with considerations of strategy) to adopt these arguments than to continually think through, for each stage in the development of capitalism, the actual unity of determinations of the social whole.

Lost sight of in the later literature is Marx's emphasis on the two issues which are at the heart of any radical critique: what is a unit, and how do units interrelate? For Marx, criticism and praxis begin precisely by questioning those units which are thought to be actually in the world, which are not thought of as creations of ideology, by showing that the placing of these units outside ideology is itself an ideological strategy. Through this strategy, units appear to have an abstract, true and therefore timeless grounding. The social formation is reproduced through restricting and bounding the range of thinkable and actable possibilities, creating a sense of inevitability, and by uniquely situating the present as the setting of apparent choice. [19]

If the ideological strategy is to present a constrained world of given, bounded possibilities, the marxist alternative is not to artificially unbound these possibilities, to imagine that they can simply be thought away, perhaps to be replaced with other possibilities. The alternative is not hedonism or decadence (which always pathetically stops short of its goal), the artificial generation of possibilities as if one can simply think one's way to any place, any time. (In fact, we later criticize this approach to ideology as "substitution," a substitution of empty form for empty form.) The point is rather to be able to focus on those limitations which make a particular social formation—here, advanced monopoly capitalism—seem inevitable (see Marchak 1975). It now appears that in order to understand those limitations for advanced monopoly capitalism, it is not enough to reiterate critiques of prior capitalist periods. In a necessarily initial analytic strategy, we need to think through the relation between analytic domains and the idea of the social whole. The correct injunction to be concrete, to do specific studies and not to repeat formulas as verities (cf. Lenin, Mao, Guevara, Cabral) is a powerful weapon for liberation, especially in the Third World. But that injunction can also obscure the point that what is concrete is also a theoretical question, especially for Euro-North American societies.

What appears to be the most concrete, is what appears to be the most autonomous, as it presents itself with an isolable, thing-like status. Since Marx, the analytic emphasis slowly has shifted from the existence of relative autonomy as a condition of the reproduction of the social formation, to analyses focussed within domains and institutions which have the appearance of an integrity of their own. To that extent, the critical edge of marxism is sacrificed to a classification of "practices," "institutions" or "sub-systems," and questions become posed ideologically, not scientifically. A sub-system (e.g., education with a school system) then seems to have its "apparatus" (e.g., the educational apparatus, the media elite etc.). The issue shifts toward how the organization of the sub-system accounts for the existence of relative autonomy, and away from how relative autonomy is itself an aspect of the unity of determinations that is the social whole. Or, the question of why sub-systems appear to have integrity is not directly raised at the beginning. [20]

*The Question of Autonomy: Orthodox Marxism.* In current orthodox marxism, the analytic project is to apply categories such as "base" and "superstructure" to concrete situations in innovative ways, but the tenuous nature of the question of the social whole is summarized by the phrase, "in the last instance." This phrase is used to characterize the determination of the superstructure by the base. It expresses the position that one cannot immediately move from a particular characterization of the base, to a very specific characterization of the superstructure. The base determines, but "in the last instance." This is a have-your-cake-and-eat-it-too maneuver, which sustains the image of an orthodox marxist determinism, while leaving open (rather than analyzing) the issue of relatively autonomous forms and institutionalizations. [21]

Orthodox marxism appears to have substituted certain words (e.g., bourgeois individualism, racism, sexism) for an understanding of ideology as form. While the words are weighted with a density of meaning tied to the history of marxism, their application in particular situations often seems weak or arbitrary. The analysis of ideology is reduced to a vocabulary where each word floats in an unnamed sea. [22]

Orthodox marxism begins with the assumption that the categories of base and superstructure are given, and analysis should proceed in terms of them. Another significant current trend in marxist analysis posits the need for a continuing critique through which categories will be generated by the progressively deeper penetration of ideological mystification. Here we have in mind aspects of cultural marxism, structural marxism, the Frankfurt school, where ideology is examined as semi-autonomous form. This starting point depends on a prior isolation of superstructure as a domain, as is the case in orthodox marxism, but a sort of alliance can be formed with the latest approaches to symbolic analysis. [23]

*The Question of Autonomy: Cultural Marxism.* In cultural marxism, ideological elements appear in a set (domain) and they are to be analyzed in relation to one another. Those interrelations exhaust the possibilities of understanding the domain, except for very general references to the embedding of the domain in a larger matrix. But here the analysis loses its inital impetus, which was the understanding of the nature of the social whole. The initial impetus is lost because to the extent to which the analysis of the domain can be exhaustive, any social whole larger than the domain becomes analytically unnecessary.

Let us be clear about the alternatives, where the question of ideology is taken seriously. One can either search for form within a set of ideological symbols, or one can see meanings in symbols as relating immediately not only to other meanings in symbols, but also as relating immediately to that unity of determinations which constitutes the social whole. This latter alternative is what we take as continuing the development of historical materialism, and is what we attempt to do concretely in the following chapters. For such an historical materialism, understanding structural tendencies requires that we include meaning both in symbolic form and in social action, in the same analytic universe. Or, phrased otherwise, such an historical materialism requires that we can question the category of ideology itself to the extent that studies of ideology as structure abstract symbolic meaning from its embeddedness within a particular social whole. (In Chapter 2, we try to show how a line of argument which develops the analysis of "cultural definitions" can be broadened to demonstrate how those definitions are linked immediately to a structure of domination which characterizes the social whole. In Chapter 3, we begin implicitly with the assumption that a theoretical demonstration of the immediacy of such links has already been made, at least for one kind of social formation.)

A provisional resolution of the continuing concern to relate meaning to context is not to search for an appropriate context which can then be taken as given so that we can proceed with the study of symbolic structures per se. We should rather see meaning in symbols as an aspect of the structure of the social whole. This avoids the dilemma of symbolic analysis that relies on the concepts of metaphor and metonymy without adequate grounding, and thus endlessly searches for the primary context (e.g., 'father' is biological pater, 'priest' as father is a "metaphorical extension"). [24] To paraphrase Gertrude Stein, a context is a context; each context reveals an aspect of the social whole.

*The Social-Epistemological Problem.* While we question the analytic ease of initially creating domains and units, we also recognize that we have no immediate difficulty in defining units and boundaries in a logical sense (A is not B). But we cannot start, or stop, with that facility. If we start or stop there, we shield ourselves from the self-reflexive question of the relation between such apparently neutral procedures (the recognition of units, boundaries, domains) and contemporary bourgeois culture. As Lukács (1971 [1922]) brilliantly suggested, the significant issue is the extent to which scientific method is taken over as a metaphor for bourgeois culture (and, we might add, vice versa).

If we look at the construction of sameness and difference (e.g., in typologies, categories) in both scientific discourse and in everyday life in advanced capitalist society, it is apparent that there are basic homologies between those constructions in everyday life and in scientific discourse. These homologies do not reflect a profound concordance with an objective reality, but rather reveal contradictions and a problematic that "crosscuts" apparently different compartments of superstructure (legal-political institutions, language, religion, etc.). We are indeed critically alerted when our common sense appears in tune with our analytic categories.

We cannot escape the fundamental problem created by the fact that analytic social thought constructs units and boundaries in the same manner as bourgeois political philosophy constructs persons and society. To state the relation in a proportion:

Bounded units : System :: Persons : Society

Persons appear as both antecedent and autonomous, yet combine to form the polity. This contradiction of independence and dependence is necessary to justify bourgeois political participation, and is the foundation of its mystification. The contradiction is reflected in the idea that analytical units are bounded so that they have a certain independence of any surrounding, yet those units are also dependent on their particular surrounding. (For example, if it is assumed that one can talk about "the family" in X, Y and Z societies, while of course recognizing that "it" is differentially conditioned in each. Or if it is assumed that one can similarly talk about base and superstructure.)

This homology between analytic social thought, bourgeois political philosophy and common sense should be precisely the

starting point of a marxist critique. It becomes an implicit part
of any marxist analysis that takes units and boundaries as givens,
as ahistorical features of a putative objective world.

We may recognize that base and superstructure are abstractions.
But we can also pursue the implications of this point: that what
is represented by each "level" cannot be completed on its own as
a form; the particular unity of what may be distinguished by the
ensemble of such theoretical levels is the simplest instance of
form. We can pursue this observation to the point of asking: how
do assumptions about domains and boundaries, derived from our
own common sense, affect our critical theorizing and praxis precisely about that common sense?

Formulating the matter in this way immediately questions the
domains of base and superstructure as having generic validity
across space and time. Formulating the matter in this way suggests
that before we fill in the content of domains which are apparently
given in the world, we must examine the idea of domains to begin
with. This is not an abstract formulation, but involves the specific
procedure of noting both the surface proliferation of domains
(and the conditions of their autonomy), and the unity of determinations that underlies both the specific proliferations and the
logic of autonomy.

This returns us to Marx, especially the Marx of *Capital* (not
only to the "young Marx"). In *Capital,* the question of domains
is raised around the issue of what is a commodity. After Marx's
death, Engels took pains to point out that the one-sided reading
of *Capital* as stressing "economic" issues obscured the total critique of capitalism that Marx intended (but did not complete; witness his outline for a volume on the State). But the method of
restoring that conceptual holism has proved elusive, occluded in
the move toward systems theory (e.g., aspects of Habermas,
Godelier), in the increasingly scholastic distinctions of structural
marxists, in the ambiguity of orthodox marxists (a little more
materialism here, a little less there). [25]

Of course, when we speak of culture or ideology, we have in
mind not simply 'high culture', but rather the content of everyday life for ordinary people. It is just this quotidian aspect which
is so troublesome in socialist states. The concern about the quotidian felt by many Western marxists is not raised in a sustained

dialogue with those living under socialism. Rather, Western marxists claim to know how to avoid certain 'errors' of socialist state
practice, but the avoidance is typically a facile assertion of "demo-
cratic values" without an actual linking of those values to marxist theory. (In fact, once again an implicit "social contract" approach emerges within aspects of marxist thought.)

*Theory and Practice.* Ideological and cultural issues move to the
periphery when the social whole is given in terms such as base and
superstructure, with superstructure analytically reduced to a set of
evocative words (e.g., bourgeois individualism, racism). This
phenomenon should be understood in the context of the immediate necessity in some places of creating socialist states, with
immediate 'economic' priorities. If one assumes that changes in
ideology lag behind changes in the base, one can then entertain
the notion that these ideological concerns will somehow, naturally, work themselves out over time, if the state has become
'socialist'. Since base is materialistically prior, ideology must
eventually come around. (Hence the liberation of women that
will 'naturally' follow the move to socialism.)

Thus the "in the last instance" mode of dealing with the relation between base and superstructure has practical consequences.
If one speaks of determination, and the determination of the
superstructure by the base is "in the last instance," one can
explain and justify either no variation in ideological forms or
essentially free variation in ideological forms. Theory weakens,
New Left fantasies about the reconstruction of culture emerge in
the West, socialist realism becomes policy in socialist countries,
without real justification in the theory to which they claim
allegiance, but with decisive consequences for everyday life.

In socialist states, formulating cultural policy beyond the
direct struggle for liberation has proved suprisingly elusive. We
have seen, for example, the tunnel vision of socialist realism and
the apparent flattening of artistic effort and struggle during recent
Chinese history. An aspect of capitalist culture appears at a certain time to be ideologically rejected as 'bourgeois' or 'decadent',
but this merely expresses time lag, as the rejected item later becomes incorporated into socialist culture. (Consider, for example,
the case of the Beatles' initial condemnation in the U.S.S.R., and
the later release of their records.)

Without taking sides, it is also fascinating that on 'political' and 'economic' issues, West European communist parties so quickly take positions previously thought to be foreign to radical praxis, and that China can almost overnight condemn previous policy ostensibly developed through mass participation.

Of course, these shifts are justified as being 'correct' from a marxist perspective. What else? And yet these decisive movements suggest a return to the question of the theoretical foundations of the marxist perspective, not simply a continuation of matters as usual.

The analysis of the place of ideology in a particular social whole has significant results in the content of socialist life, and for the prospects of socialist transformation, yet that analysis is a weak one. We cannot account for this weakness by appealing to inherent analytic difficulties, or to the supposed peripheral role of ideological questions in organizing for transformation. Rather, the potentially subversive nature of such analysis is dangerous. Just as within anthropology we are increasingly concerned about the basic question of what is the same and what is different, as we become aware of the extent to which we analytically carry over constructions basic to our own society, within marxism there is increasing uncertainty about what is radical criticism, in contrast to criticism which masks the justification of existing conditions.

In advanced capitalist states (especially the U.S.), the left agitates as usual (over so-called economic, bread and butter issues) without an emphasis on ideological oppression, and without much success (but with the old promise that "the number of strikes is increasing"). The left attempts to reach larger numbers by bracketing the left critique of bourgeois lifestyles that have penetrated the working class quotidian.

It seems that people on the left think that they need not stress ideological oppression since it will wither away under socialism, or that ideological oppression is dangerous to stress since such an emphasis would 'turn off' potential sympathizers by too quickly intruding into the content of their everyday lives. Alternatively still, the left may defiantly proclaim ideological oppression (in what amounts to a cliché), although it does in fact 'turn off' many workers (e.g., the problems of opposing racism in a factory).

The ease with which West European communist parties shift

their positions is only matched by the ease with which American left factions so easily reciprocally label each other as 'racist'.

While in the socialist states the notion of the vanguard becomes bureaucratically reified, in advanced capitalist states the left seems to be abandoning a vanguard role for what Lenin termed tailism.

Of course, the argument should not be used to discount the efforts of those who in significant ways are 'putting themselves on the line' for genuinely progressive causes. But at some point these dilemmas must be faced, since only by facing them can people put themselves on the line in a way that continually interrelates theory and practice.

Given the shifts of position in the socialist states, and the changeable sloganeering of Western left factions, we see a slow-motion agglutination of contradictory marxist positions. Its theoretical consequences are a stagnation of marxist thought as it applies to advanced capitalist society (versus the heightened relevance of marxism in colonial and neo-colonial struggle). We also see a flaccidity at the heart of radical praxis in advanced capitalist society: Western marxists typically live within a contradiction of arguing an overthrow of capitalist oppression, while deriving significant sustenance not only from the 'material' things which are tied to that same capitalism, but also from the 'cultural' forms which are tied to it. This is an important contradiction, for it goes to the heart of the marxist program: the social whole as the starting point of dialectical understanding. Many Western marxists have a scissors and paste approach: cut this out, paste that here, without relating these snippets to a social whole.

The issue of the creation and placement of domains or units is thus an issue which surfaces in theory and in practice, in marxism and in anthropology, in everyday life as it is lived and as its reconstruction is formulated. One way of describing the issue is as the process of reification. Marx profoundly analyzed the reification of things as the model for human relations, in the abbreviated section on commodity fetishism in the first volume of *Capital*. This analysis has itself become a model to be followed, as marxists have discussed the significant reifications in various stages of capitalism. But the problem of reification raises another problem which is sometimes lost sight of: what is the alternative to reification?

This issue is suggested by Marx and Engels in *The German Ideology*, when they wistfully speak of a free substitution of tasks for the socialist individual (e.g., hunting in the morning, fishing in the afternoon, criticizing after dinner). Lenin elaborated the matter when he counterposed an unthinkable flux as being the only alternative to categorization itself.

The formulation goes something like this: in a communist society, each person can choose temporary reifications, or states of being, while moving freely among various options. (The brutalized reifications needed to reproduce capitalist society would slowly fade away as their necessity faded.) The relations between such states of being are not perceived on the model of the relations between things, but nonetheless there is more here than the simple avoidance of objectification by the transparent maneuver of constant subjectification. That grants a continuing priority to objectification since it negatively characterizes its opposite. Something changes, the system reproducing the compulsion of present reifications. But something also remains the same, the basic structure of bounded domains with the person as the agent of choice.

There is genuine conceptual advancement here, compared to a presentation of self in terms of objectification, in terms of consumer choice, and even in terms of personal needs, but the construction of the "communist" individual still appears to retain features tied to the Enlightenment philosophical concept of the polity as being constituted by a social contract. In a sense, the retention of too much of the content of the Enlightenment concept of the individual obscures the possibilities of recognizing the dialectic creativity of future social formations. We are suggesting that the individual of *The German Ideology* can be still further criticized and embedded in capitalism, and that this criticism depends upon the ideological homology between the person as constituted within a system of constructions that legitimize the 'liberal' State, and the nature of domains and boundaries that underlie both our common sense and, to a great extent, our social theorizing. Focusing on this point allows us to reraise the nature of the social whole in advanced capitalist society and to explore, in the next chapter, the individual in contemporary Euro-American 'liberal' ideology.

This simplified version of communist possibilities should appear somewhat unsettling, for what it brackets epistemologically and for its consequences in contemporary socialist states. The version still takes each reification (domain) in itself, without seeking an overall form, and hence must regard certain units as being actual even if they are temporary. (As Lenin suggested, one cannot live in an undifferentiated flux.) Furthermore, the person, not as the "bourgeois individual" so easily dissected in marxist literature but still as a symbolic unit and not simply a biological entity, remains the locus of value, the entity which is the warrant for one choice or another.

Once we accept it as being given that base and superstructure are initially separable analytic starting points (i.e., only later do we treat their interpenetration) and once we locate the individual as a necessary agent of choice, we guarantee an understanding of reification that moves between the alienation of capitalist society, and the abstract sequencing of alternatives in socialist society. And, crucially, we lose the essential marxist thrust: criticize everything that contributes to the reproduction of capitalist society. We lose the thrust as we reify the relative autonomy of the categories base, superstructure and person, at the expense of starting with a consideration of the social whole. These units become actual, not simply ideological units, and so the relations among them are to be "discovered." Crucially, it is as though real persons make real ideological choices, say to eat oatmeal or cornflakes, and the only remaining question to be answered is how these real people make these real choices. One may take the view that if capitalism is ended, the choices can be made 'freely' without the underlying distortion of profit making, but the choices are choices nonetheless given capitalism or socialism. In either case, persons choose among units and types. It is just this obviousness that we critically discuss in this volume. The obviousness is that if we remove surplus value, the basic proportion (bounded units : system :: person : society) still stands. What we are trying to do is to question the construction of the elements of the proportion.

The fallacy of misplaced concreteness which expresses the current confusion over the alternatives of reification versus flux, orients us toward foundations. Current marxist discourse sets up particular options as separate possibilities, just as bourgeois political philosophy posits competition among distinct, equivalent persons. In contemporary capitalist society, the reproduction of the social formation (from the aspect of the reproduction of labor power) takes place as an oscillation among these so-called separate possibilities or choices, where each choice is seen as real, not as emerging only in comparison with related choices. When a balloon is squeezed in one place, it expands in another, and it would be foolish to try to find the one place to squeeze that would not cause expansion elsewhere. Radical action, taken as finding the correct line among particular bounded choices (prefigured in capitalist ideology), follows the balloon analogy for it involves searching for the 'correct line' at the level of units already reified within contemporary advanced capitalism. The fallacy of misplaced concreteness is expressed in the notion that these units can bear the load of action and choice. Against this, we suggest that the relations among such units, rather than the boundedness and the analytic autonomy of each unit, form the basis for a radical critique and a radical praxis; that one has to unbound units and perceive them as determinations within a genuine social whole to provide the starting point for understanding reification.

The problem for radical action must, at certain moments, become recognized as the problem of what is radical itself, rather than only a matter of tactics given allegedly clear goals and a profound sense of necessity. If we can crudely summarize three such moments: for Marx's time, for Lenin's, and for our own, we can more closely see the problems in present neo-marxist methods and the need to question previous givens to reset the ability to act in the world.

Marx saw radical action as deriving from the working class as a whole acting in its class interest. Base relations situated that interest through the extraction of surplus-value, and workers could be made directly aware, through agitation and workingmen's associations, of the necessity for class action to overthrow that private ownership internally related to market-based economic exchange, and the social formation built up around that form of exchange. Here the link between superstructure and base through the person is clear: superstructure is opaque; unlike pre-capitalist ideology, it conceals and mystifies base relations, but that mystification can be rejected by the working class as a class.

Experience and the changing nature of capitalism made it clear to Lenin that without the development of a vanguard party, the development of the working class as a class was limited to "trade union consciousness." While base, superstructure and the person remained analytically prior units, the idea of the person as a class actor rather than as an individual actor became coincident with the vanguard communist party. Although the units retained reality, their placement and significance altered as the immediate problem of the creation of the first socialist state was characterized in terms of economic factors and necessities ("defense of socialism at all costs").

But advanced monopoly capitalism is not the capitalism of Lenin. For the purposes of understanding ideological issues in the United States and some other western capitalist nations, the decisive movement has been the integration of marketing techniques (through advertising and product differentiation) with the ideology of bourgeois self-definition and self-development. By identifying the self with what is produced and by marketing products designed to sell on the basis of a continuous substitution of self-images, an aspect of production is transformed to the "production of signs" (Baudrillard 1972, 1975) and artificial production (based on style and planned obsolescence) is generated which at least ameliorates the problem of the "absorption of surplus" in capitalist systems (Baran and Sweezy 1968).

Thus we are suggesting that ideological developments in advanced monopoly capitalism, at least in the places where ownership is concentrated, go along with a decisive change in what is produced, how products are sold, and the relation of consumption patterns to the construction of the self. We further suggest that this decisive change immediately relates to a classic issue in a marxist theory of economic crises in capitalism—the generating and absorption of an economic surplus. Crucially, this shift in patterns of production also alters the previous immediacy (but not centrality) of class-based ideological forms to the extent that it implicates all persons in a generalized structure of substitution and domination. This does not negate the idea of class struggle but it does imply a re-situating of "class" in contemporary ideology, a re-situating that permits one to see class issues emerging within this generalized ideological configuration. Hence we feel that as a necessary first step in rethinking marxist approaches to superstructure, we can start with an analysis of ideology in its relations with the most global practices. The next chapter is such a step and so we *assume* a shift in forms of production relating to the matter of absorption and *we do not fully develop* the analysis of class questions. In that sense, this effort should be read as the beginning of a "genetic structural" study of advanced capitalist ideology that is our long-range project (see Piaget 1950, Goldmann 1977).

The significance of the integration of marketing techniques with the ideology of bourgeois self-definition and self-development is that it defines a social formation in which bounded units exist but which may be substituted for each other, and where that substitution is linked to a particular notion of the self and of the possibilities of that self. The purchase of a car, clothing, etc., all reflect (or are made to seem to reflect) aspects of the self, and if one purchase does not work, another purchase may be substituted for it in the same quest for self-realization. The system is characterized by the movement among such units, the differences among those units relating immediately to one another rather than to some entity outside them. The system is not decisively characterized by the nature of any unit taken in itself. This holds true for superstructure, where to be internal to the system is to take units and boundaries as given, and then to move among them (whether in buying a car or in choosing among radical lines). [26]

Therefore, to the extent that radical theory and praxis still reifies the person as a unit and still poses the interpenetration of base and superstructure as a secondary analytic level, it has been superseded and encompassed by a capitalism that can use such units and such separations to reproduce itself, since the loss of the social whole presages a loss of the marxist critical edge, to marxism as systems theory or ego psychology. And radicals fall into the trap of trying this, then that, endlessly squeezing the balloon, while the task is to examine the balloon itself, to return to the social whole as it is presently given, to return to the question of what is reification and what is radical action.

If this is not realized, one endlessly searches for the correct line on classism, ageism, racism or sexism as such, rather than seeing the capitalist imprint on the very existence of those units, given as internal liberal equivalents. Practically, the effects of such a search for a correct line are that capitalism flourishes and radicals become discouraged.

In Marx's time, ideology was linked to the base to the extent that the extraction of surplus-value was concealed and private property was made to appear natural, thus transforming relations between persons to relations between things. For us, our very notion of self and self-identity are tied to production and market processes designed to sell us a range of products. That link between self-identity and consumption, as fashion, not as simply having more of a thing, was not given in Marx's time when the issue was more one of how a thing was produced, not of what was to be produced. This specific interpenetration of ideology and production is what makes their previous separation, while significant for penetrating a previous social whole, inadequate for advanced monopoly capitalism.

To put the matter simply and bluntly: if one goes into a shop to buy something which defines oneself and is watched by a licensed security guard, there is something very important going on. The unity of the aspects of this 'act' in everyday life should not be obscured by modes of analysis which make those aspects appear as though they emanate from different "levels" or "regions" of some rarefied "structure."[27]

It is not only that people may define themselves by their styles of consumption or that we are, more or less, victimized by "hidden persuaders." What is possible is that the person's reality becomes increasingly defined in terms of the 'markets' in which the person participates (the sports market, the young-marrieds market, the sex market, the ethnic market), and that reality has the potential of suffering as the contradictions inherent in monopoly capitalist accumulation are realized in those markets. Production is still the decisive moment, as it was for Marx. Ideological construction must still deal with failures in the system, but with failures over a wider range of life activity.

With the apparent increasingly erratic nature of prices and the erratic availability of specific jobs and consumer goods, the taken-for-grantedness of mediating institutions (e.g., 'the market') may no longer be so taken-for-granted. It becomes more possible to diagnose the source of the difficulty as being other than abstract, mysterious forces (e.g., 'supply and demand'), and perhaps to locate those sources more concretely (Exxon, Weston Foods). Indeed, the relation between the importance of marketing, the market appropriation of the self, monopoly pricing and monopoly regulation of the availability of commodities is itself an internal relation. But here again, the attention can be directed away from the social whole and toward particular units of production. Such an identification may be very progressive (e.g., in asserting control over one's dominated national economy), but that identification can also be absorbed by locating such entities within a now enlarged, partially substitutable family of negative forces: Exxon, Weston Foods, the State, the Winter, low productivity and so forth. Since these phenomena are otherwise regarded as being phenomena at different levels or as having to do with different sorts of things, it is no wonder that a certain amount of confusion prevails as to how the world works!

If the reproduction of contemporary capitalist society is tied not simply to specific categories, but to the very way we categorize, we need corresponding approaches that start from the problem of categorization. It is important to keep in mind that recognizing the problem of categorization as central emerges not only from general analytic interests, but also from problems of radical action. From the side of problems of radical action, the question is how to choose, how to act and who are those who are the actors. Even using the category 'revolution', timelessly repeated by radicals, is elusive in this context, given its appropriation by capitalism (practically anything can constitute a revolution in anything, from soup to countries) and given the lack of attention to the unity of determinations within which we operate.

CONCLUSION

From the analytic side, we need not outline a specific program here. Colleagues, at least, may accept the strategy of a "starting point." But we must return to the prior stage of understanding what a program could look like, not to avoid questions of praxis, but to avoid reproducing existing conditions through programs which intend to change them. This becomes our problem, the concern around which we concentrate our analysis: why has contemporary radical action failed to escape being encompassed by capitalism, and how can we begin to criticize (as one aspect of a larger praxis) profoundly enough to escape that encompassment?

Our first approximation is that earlier marxist modes of

analysis are not sufficient to the extent that they depend upon units and categories internal to advanced monopoly capitalism, a capitalism the internal lineaments of which have significantly changed in the past 50 years. Orthodox marxism searches for the correct line, basing itself on a materialism which foregrounds base and relegates superstructure to a secondary place. Any line derived from such a starting point is ultimately not actable in advanced capitalist contexts and does not significantly affect opinion. Cultural marxism searches for ideological structures at the level of symbolic meaning as such. This, too, separates thought and action in a way congenial to the reproduction of capitalism. If, after all, ideological analysis is complete on its own level, then action is redundant, imitative or absurd. Both orthodox marxism and cultural marxism in advanced capitalist societies have lost the sense of a social whole that animates marxist praxis.

By avoiding abstract formulations of categories, either innocently attached to our own (as in the idea of the family or kinship) or more subtly attached to capitalist reproduction (as in the idea of 'making a contribution to society'), we start instead with the specific problem of contemporary radical action. There we see the issue of the social whole as being posed by the lack of completeness of any "structure" (economic, ideological, social) taken at its own level, as either a real or an analytically viable category or subsystem. Structure for us emerges precisely at the point where such units, categories and boundaries result in contradictions, either between thought and action, or levels of thought or levels of action: that is, where categorization fails, where the attempt to statically order the world emerges as ideology. Such structures are formed in praxis and are analyzable only in terms of that praxis, both as relative success and as relative failure. Reifications in this framework are the consequence of seeing form as being packed into bounded units. Forms emerge not as things but as moments of struggle, defined by past struggle and shaping future struggle. It is not a matter of hunting in the morning and criticizing at night, but of asking what hunting or criticizing are, as states or objects. One can take the passage in Marx and Engels as making this point, and we are continuing that aspect of marxism.

These concerns are similar in one way to the anthropological problem of sameness and difference, since in both we have come to realize our dependence on our own problematic and the extreme difficulty of distancing ourselves from that problematic. In both critical anthropology and neomarxist thought, the creative step is to start with a social whole as given at a particular moment, to resist the imposition of either specific categories, or, more subtly, of our own idea of categorization upon it.

The problems of sameness vs. difference, of independence vs. dependence (or phrased differently: of part and whole) and of justification vs. critique are situated through the general analytic impasse of categorization in social thought. The initial breakdown into analytic domains increasingly seems to lead us into conundrums which have the flavor of antinomies. Either side, taken as a side, can be argued equally well or poorly: history/structure, reification/flux, thought/action, domains/social whole, base/superstructure. One can either continue the argument on behalf of one side or another, or one can suggest that the present form of these oppositions poses a central analytic question, as was suggested toward the end of the last section. In the following chapters we develop ways of starting with the issue of antinomies by rejecting their structure as such, and by focusing on contradictions generated when the terms of the antinomies are seen as analytically viable categories. By seeing these categories as ideological, not scientific, we are continuing historical materialism through a rethinking of what is a scientific question when applied to human social formations. And by focusing on everyday life, we seek to restore a dimension restricted both in marxism and in anthropology. Our data derive from ordinary situations and mundane constructions, not elaborate rituals or great novels.

The following chapters should be taken as explorations with this approach. We attempt to study other societies without immediately imposing our own categories, and to use the insights developed through that study to criticize the forms of categorization basic to our problematic.

# SEPARATIONS IN CAPITALIST SOCIETIES: PERSONS, THINGS, UNITS AND RELATIONS

In *The German Ideology*, Marx (1970a [1846] :86) observes the historical nature of the "... difference between the individual as a person and what is accidental to him...." When social relations correspond to productive forces, these relations are seen as uniquely real by the actors, as part of their personal activity and surrounding world. But those social relations which are survivals of previous modes of production appear external to the actor. Those relations appear as accidental states or obstacles. In this chapter we will develop, and modify, the distinction by discussing two forms of ideological domination: personal domination and abstracted domination. Personal domination (the domination of persons by persons) appears as accidental. Once recognized (in the case of racism, sexism, etc.), it seems as if it can be eradicated within the system, but programs for eradication, confidently begun, soon falter and their failure must be explained away. Abstracted domination (the domination of something separable from the person by something separable from a person; most clearly, class domination) appears as the 'real world' and so is not recognized as domination. (Of course, there is a movement between personal domination and abstracted domination, which we will discuss below.[1] )

We will argue that these two modes of ideological domination are interrelated aspects of a complex structure within which often implicit assumptions are made about the nature of individuals or persons and about things related to persons. We suggest that these assumptions are most clearly articulated in an historic ideological transformation which is part of the development of modern capitalism.

We will pursue the implications of this transformation in an apparently roundabout way. First, after a quick look at Sir Henry Maine and a few references to contemporary social science interest in 'the individual', we will look at the construction of domains (kinship, work, nationality, religion) in capitalist ideology through Schneider's *American Kinship* and a later article (D.M. Schneider 1968, 1970). Then we will see how the structural relations between these domains provide a key to understanding how individualism and the cultural construction of natural substances operate as forms which underlie contemporary ideological domination in many parts of the West. Analysis of the structural relations brings us finally to Marx's understanding of use-value, exchange-value, the fetishism of commodities and alienation.

We draw attention to the contrast between meanings associated with: (1) kinship, nationality, and religion on the one hand, and (2) contract on the other. We explore the different constructions of substance and social action in (1) and (2). We suggest that substantialized symbolism is the symbolism of personal domination, whereas contractualized symbolism is the symbolism of abstracted domination, and we explore the role of the State in this system of relations.

The contrast between personal and abstracted domination corresponds to the distinction between the individual, and that which is separable from the individual. The ideologically 'fully individual' individual is not just any person, however, but is rather a person who dominates and who is dominated in a particular way. People who are personally dominated are ideologically represented as being substantially incomplete or defective; they are represented as being less-than-full individuals. This appearance can be used to perpetuate and explain both personal and abstracted domination. In the ideology, these substantializations (e.g., race and sex, which are posed as being aspects of biological substance) become substitutable for one another in particular ways. Forces which are invoked to justify action (e.g., God, Nature) also become substitutable for one another in particular ways.

The possibility of these substitutions can be seen in the context of the entire repertoire of substitutions which occur within capitalist formations.

The paradigmatic individual is a relational monad: isolated from others, yet necessarily implicated in their action.

THE QUESTION OF THE INDIVIDUAL

The movement of the progressive societies has been uniform in one respect. Through all its course it has been distinguished by the gradual dissolution of family dependency and the growth of individual obligation in its place. The individual is steadily substituted for the Family, as the unit of which civil laws take account. The advance has been accomplished by varying rates of celerity, and there are societies not absolutely stationary in which the collapse of the ancient organization can only be perceived by careful study of the phenomena they present. But, whatever its pace, the change has not been subject to reaction or recoil, and apparent retardations will be found to have been occasioned through the absorption of archaic ideas and customs from some entirely foreign source. Nor is it difficult to see what is the tie between man and man which replaces by degrees those forms of reciprocity in rights and duties which have their origin in the Family. It is Contract. Starting, as from one terminus of history, from a condition of society in which all the relations of Persons are summed up in the relations of Family, we seem to have steadily moved towards a phase of social order in which all these relations arise from the free agreement of individuals. In Western Europe the progress achieved in this direction has been considerable. Thus the status of the Slave has disappeared—it has been superseded by the contractual relation of the servant to his master. The status of the Female under Tutelage, if the tutelage be understood of persons other than her husband, has also ceased to exist; from her coming of age to her marriage all the relations she may form are relations of contract. So too the status of the Son under Power has no true place in the law of modern European societies. If any civil obligation bind together the Parent and the child of full age, it is one to which only contract gives its legal validity. The apparent exceptions are exceptions of that stamp which will illustrate the rule. The child before years of discretion, the orphan under guardianship, the adjudged lunatic, have all their capacities and incapacities regulated by the Law of Persons. But why? The reason is differently expressed in the conventional language of different systems, but in substance it is stated to the same effect by all. The great majority of Jurists are constant to the principle that the classes of persons just mentioned are subject to extrinsic control on the single ground that they do not possess the faculty of forming a judgment on their own interests; in other words, that they are wanting in the first essential of an engagement by Contract.

The word Status may be usefully employed to construct a formula expressing the law of progress thus indicated, which, whatever be its value, seems to me to be sufficiently ascertained. All the forms of Status taken notice of in the Law of Persons were derived from, and to some extent are still colored by, the powers and privileges anciently residing in the Family. If then we employ Status, agreeably with the usage of the best writers, to signify these personal conditions only, and avoid applying the term to such conditions as are the immediate or remote result of agreement, we may say that the movement of the progressive societies has hitherto been a movement *from Status to Contract* (Maine 1970[1884]: 163-165; emphasis in the original).

So wrote Sir Henry Sumner Maine in *Ancient Law* (first edition published in 1861).[2] And on the same theme:

There are few general propositions concerning the age to which we belong which seem at first sight likely to be received with readier concurrence than the assertion that the society of our day is mainly distinguished from that of preceding generations by the largeness of the sphere which is occupied in it by Contract. Some of the phenomena on which this proposition rests are among those most frequently singled out for notice, for comment, and for eulogy. Not many of us are so unobservant as not to perceive that in innumerable cases where old law fixed a man's social position irreversibly at his birth, modern law allows him to create it for himself by convention; and indeed several of the few exceptions which remain to this rule are constantly denounced with passionate indignation. The point, for instance, which is really debated in the vigorous controversy still carried on upon the subject of negro servitude, is whether the status of slave does not belong to by-gone institutions, and whether the only relation between employer and labourer which commends itself to modern morality be not a relation determined exclusively by contract. The recognition of this difference between past ages and the present enters into the very essence of the most famous contemporary speculations. It is certain that the science of Political Economy, the only department of moral inquiry which has made any considerable progress in our day, would fail to correspond with the facts of life if it were not true that Imperative Law had abandoned the largest part of the field which it once occupied, and had left men to settle rules of conduct for themselves with a liberty never allowed to them till recently. The bias indeed of most persons trained in political economy is to consider the general truth on which their science reposes as entitled to become universal, and, when they apply it as an art, their efforts are ordinarily directed to enlarging the province of Contract and to curtailing that of Imperative Law, except so far as law is necessary to enforce the performance of Contracts (Maine 1970 [1884] :295-296).

The kind of contrast Maine draws is echoed in the more contemporary social science distinction between "ascribed" and "achieved" status.[3] The latter contrast can perform the double service of appearing to be applicable in all forms of society, while at the same time locating the Western analyst at the pinnacle of the evolution of freedom.[4] Part of the point of the contrast seems to quiver as studies of mobility and elites in Western capitalist countries conclude that, often enough, rags is the child of rags, and riches the child of riches (e.g., Clement 1975, Parkin 1971).

However, the issue of the comparative interpretation of the 'individual' and corresponding aspects of the forms of social relations has now resurfaced from a number of related directions: Dumont's papers on individualism and holism, from which we draw heavily (Dumont 1961, 1965, 1970, 1971); D.M. Schneider's work on American kinship and related matters; the so-called marxist revival in Western social science (e.g., see Meillassoux 1972).

## SCHNEIDER ON AMERICAN KINSHIP: FROM KINSHIP TO HOME AND WORK.... TO CONTRACT.... TO THE CAPITALIST MODE OF PRODUCTION

In *American Kinship*, Schneider (1968) identifies two meanings or aspects of kinship, at least for the American urban white middle class. As a relationship, kinship appears as one which has to do with natural substance. As a relationship, kinship also appears as one which has to do with a "code for conduct." Relationship as natural substance is relationship by blood, which is culturally defined as a fact of nature. Relationship as "code for conduct" is relationship as a social relationship, the content of which Schneider describes as being that of "enduring, diffuse solidarity." "Enduring" indicates that the relationship is not a transient one, but is a permanent one. "Diffuse" indicates that the relationship is not specified in terms of particular social acts which are necessary for the relationship to exist. The claims of relatives (as relatives) upon one another are open, unspecified.

Schneider indicates that there is an implicit categorization of relatives into three categories: (1) relatives by blood: people who share both (culturally defined) biological substance and a relation in law; these people are most unambiguously 'relatives'; (2) relatives in nature: people who share (culturally defined) biological substance, but not the 'legal' relation (e.g., the 'natural parent' and the 'illegitimate child'); (3) relatives in law only: e.g., spouses, who do not share biological substance; these are most ambiguously 'relatives'.

Schneider understands the contrast between substance and code for conduct as being a variation on the same theme as the contrast between nature and law. In both cases, a contrast is being drawn between that which is (allegedly) part of nature, and that which is an instance of the exercise of human law, reason or custom.

One of Schneider's major contributions to kinship studies is to identify the connection between such aspects of kinship as these, and more general cultural or cosmological categories.

Schneider also sets out the cultural paradox: (1) human activity is at one level apart from nature and acts upon nature; 'man' is regarded as being apart from nature, as human beings are regarded as being apart from animals; (2) however, human activity is at another level part of nature, and acts within nature; 'man' can be regarded as part of nature, as human beings can be regarded as a variety of animal.

Thus, on the one hand, 'the family' can be postulated as a unit in nature (deer have families, little birds have families). On the other hand, action in the family supposedly necessitates the conscious human surpressing of certain natural (perhaps, in an earlier age, devilish) impulses (sexuality between husband and wife is enjoined, but not 'animal-like' sexuality; children must be controlled by their parents lest they be 'wild'; the 'natural possibility' of incest must be forefended by separating sons' and daughters' sleeping places).

And: On the one hand, the relation between mother and child is seen as having a natural basis. But on the other hand, a mother should bring up her child in ways that reflect the applications of human knowledge (even out of manuals written by experts on child raising).

In his discussion, Schneider contrasts the enduring diffuse solidarity of kinship (and nationality, religion; see below) with the sorts of relations which apply elsewhere in American society: relations which are not permanent, and which are more clearly specified in terms of the obligations which they involve. Indeed, one may see the contrasting relations as relations of contract. [5]

The contrast becomes clearest through the following route: the paradigmatic instance of kinship is 'the family', consisting of parents and children living together. Where they live together is 'a home', and it is love which makes a house a home. Two kinds of love follow from the two kinds of relationships: cognatic love, which is the love between people linked by common substance;

and erotic love, which is the love between spouses, who are the paradigmatic relatives in law. The cultural construction of sexual intercourse provides a link between these two kinds of love, and between the kinds of relatives. The act of sexual intercourse in marriage symbolizes the relationship between spouses, and it also creates relationship by common substance through the procreation of children who are believed to have the biological substance of both parents.

'Home' contrasts with 'work'. In a later article, Schneider (1970) summarizes his point:

> Finally, the contrast between home and work brings out aspects which complete the picture of the distinctive features of kinship in American culture. This can best be understood in terms of the contrast between love and money which stand for home and work. Indeed, what one does at home, it is said, one does for love, not for money, while what one does at work one does strictly for money, not for love. Money is material, it is power, it is impersonal and universalistic, unqualified by considerations of sentiment and morality. Relations of work and money are temporary, transient, contingent. Love on the other hand is highly personal and particularistic, and beset with considerations of sentiment and morality. Where love is spiritual, money is material. Where love is enduring and without qualification, money is transient and contingent. And finally, it is personal considerations which are paramount in love—who the person is, not how well he performs, while with work and money it does not matter who he is, but only how well he performs his task. Money is in this sense impersonal (Schneider 1970: 119).

Others have used Schneider's analysis in the study of nonwestern societies (e.g., Silverman 1971), finding the concepts of natural substance and code for conduct useful elsewhere. But generally speaking, one matter has slipped by our notice. In the American case, the relationship of enduring diffuse solidarity is defined *in contrast to* other sorts of relations, relations which can be considered as relations of contract.

An important question, then, is this: could one have precisely the same meanings for something like enduring diffuse solidarity where it does *not* contrast with the kind of notion of contract which seems rather widespread in western societies? More narrowly, assuming that people do construct social relations in this contrastive fashion, if X and Y are contrasted as ways of relating and X is not contract in the American (western?) sense, could Y be enduring diffuse solidarity?   Given Schneider's assumptions about the connections between definitions, the possibility seems very unlikely.

Our attention is especially drawn to the association between family and home, between work and money, and to the opposition between the two sets. As far as we know, this specific differentiation of 'home' and 'work'—and thus, by implication, of kinship and contract—is not universal. It is characteristic of societies in which the capitalist mode of production prevails.

That is, within the capitalist mode of production, a distinction is created between work (as labor power) as production for exchange-value, and the production of use-values at home.[6] (Working in a factory is really 'work'. Is 'housework' really 'work' in the same sense?) The fact that Marx separates labor (the person's concrete work activity) from labor power (the capacity to work, which is alienated to the capitalist) points to the emergence of a domain of contract which is apart from the home.

Schneider's analysis thus points us in a particular direction. First, Schneider's analysis moves us from thinking about kinship as an autonomous domain to thinking about kinship in relation to more highly generalized cultural definitions. Second, Schneider's analysis points us to raising the question of the sort of historical society in which the capitalist mode of production prevails. Stated otherwise: in order to understand the cultural construction of kinship, we have to understand the cultural construction of contract, and vice-versa. In order to understand both, we have to understand the nature of the prevalence of the capitalist mode of production.[7]

FROM KINSHIP TO NATIONALITY AND RELIGION

Tracing the route of this connection is complex, but its facts are very concrete. Schneider provides many of the clues in a subsequent article, "Kinship, nationality and religion in American culture: toward a definition of kinship" (D.M. Schneider 1970). The difference between our analyses is that Schneider does not pursue the matter very far beyond the connection between kinship and general cultural definitions. We link Schneider's observations to observations on the mode of production in general.

Schneider is trying to demonstrate that what characterizes the structure of the kinship domain is not some fact about kinship per se, but is rather an exemplification of general cultural definitions which are also exemplified in constructs of nationality and religion. He writes:

> In American culture, one is "An American" either by birth or through a process which is called, appropriately enough, "naturalization." In precisely the same terms as kinship, there are the same two "kinds of citizens", those by birth and those by law. And indeed it would not be hard to show that the same three categories [relatives in nature (e.g., illegitimate child), relatives in law (e.g., spouses), relatives by blood (e.g., parents)] are derived from those elements. There is the person who is by birth an American but who has taken the citizenship of another country; there is a person who is American by naturalization but not by birth; and there is the person who by both birth and law is American.

> What is the role of a national? To love his country, his father- or motherland. Loyalty and support for his nation and all those who belong to it. Patriotism in the extreme of "My Country Right or Wrong" is one statement of it. But even where it does not take that particular form, loyalty to and love for one's country is the most generalized expression of diffuse enduring solidarity (D.M. Schneider 1970: 121).

Schneider does not point to a unique central symbol (e.g., territory, flag or constitution) for the nation or State, which would be the homologue of sexual intercourse in kinship. We would not expect the State to be substantialized in *precisely* the same way as kinship is, for reasons we will take up below.

But we are familiar with a variety of substantializations (in the extended sense of the term to be adumbrated shortly) of the nation or State. These substantializations include 'blood' (X blood spilling on the battlefields of Y); 'the people' (the X people); territory; and to use one of the categories of political and philosophical arguments, 'the general will'.

These substantializations of the nation or State can be seen to take a number of related forms: for example, as substance which is internal to the individual (blood), as substance in a sense partitioned to individuals (a national 'spirit'), as substance continuous with individuals (territory).

We have had a brief look at the apparently different domains of kinship and nationality. What, then, of religion, at least in the sense of the "Judeo-Christian tradition?"

With Christianity, as is well known, the criterion for membership shifted [from Judaism] from birth to volition. That is, in the most general sense, one is a Christian by an act of faith and not an act of birth, and correspondingly conversion to The Faith beomes a very different matter and a real possibility since it takes only an act of will to effect.

But this view leaves out two very important facts. Being a Jew is not simply being born a Jew. There is a code of conduct which is linked to the fact of birth. What is true is that it is the act of birth which has the quality of the defining feature, and so the other element tends to be easily overlooked. And it is here that the parallel between kinship and religion in Judaism is quite clear, for in both there are those two features, relationship as substance and relationship as code for conduct; the substance element is bio-genetic, the code for conduct is one of diffuse enduring solidarity.

Although the shift from Judaism to Christianity seems to drop the condition of substance as the defining feature and rest it entirely on the commitment to the code for conduct, this is not really so. Certainly there is a shift away from the particularistic, bio-genetic, criterion of substance as the defining feature. But the shift entails a realignment so that commitment to the code for conduct becomes paramount as the defining feature, and the substantive element is redefined from a material to a spiritual form. It is the triumph of spirit over matter that is at issue here. Closely linked to this is the prominent place given to love as a symbol, to the spiritual aspects of love, and to the spiritual aspects of creation as against its rather more narrowly material or bio-genetic aspects in Judaism.

The prevalence of the symbol of "love" in Christianity, the prevalence of the use of kinship terms in Christianity, the importance of such concepts as "faith" and "trust" and "belief" all testify, to me at least, that the domain of religion may well be structured in the same terms as kinship and nationality, and the historical fact that Judaism is indeed so clearly defined as one nation, one religion and one family suggests to me that there may be something in what I say.

Let me add one more point. If Judaism is the clearest and simplest case where kinship, religion and nationality are all a single domain, then the transformation of Christianity centers on the separation of a natural and supernatural element, so that kinship becomes differentiated as being based on relationship as natural substance, religion as relationship as supernatural (spiritual) substance. In other words, kinship and religion are more highly differentiated in Christianity than in Judaism, and this differentiation depends on a different form of the distinction between supernatural and natural (D.M. Schneider 1970:122-123, footnote omitted).

Thus Schneider argues that what we often see as different and separated domains (kinship, nationality, religion) are structured in the same way when we inspect the codes for conduct—what is implied by affiliation with the collectivities which exist in terms of such domains.

Schneider's argument goes much further than a simple functional argument does. In a simple functional argument, one might say that religion reinforces kinship, or kinship reinforces religion, or both. Schneider's point is more subtle, because of the suggestion that what might appear as different functional variables (e.g., kinship, religion) are really variations of the same themes.

## SUBSTANTIALIZATION AND CONTRACTUALIZATION

Let us call the sort of symbolism involved in ideas such as natural substance (in the kinship instance: blood) substantialized symbolism (see S. Barnett 1976, 1977; Dumont 1961, 1970).[8] Substantialized symbolism is the symbolism of things which people believe to be real things, which are in an important sense thought to be internal to the individual or continuous with the individual as a concrete being.

Substantialized symbolism is thus quintessentially ideological in nature, for it posits the ground of social relations as being real and natural, and thus non-ideological. We must try to think substantialized symbolism with Marx's model of thinking commodities in mind.

We will contrast substantialized symbolism with contractualized symbolism. Contractualized symbolism involves notions about individuals (more or less) freely entering into agreements to do certain things in accordance with certain standards or rules. Contractualized symbolism appears most clearly in the 'marketplace'. It is in the 'marketplace' that the worker sells his or her labor power. His or her ability to perform is at issue, not his or her substance or essence, since that performing is the basis of a wage which allows the extraction of surplus-value. The ideological separation of the person's performance from the person's substance structures the possibility that actors in the marketplace can be regarded as occupying equivalent positions. The acknowledgment of substance is a prior condition for entry into the marketplace in the sense that the individual is a substance. But that substance does not determine the specifics of performance in particular contexts. And so, this separation grounds the mystification of wage labor as the just reward for work, since all parties to a contract are free and equal (having the same human substance), and each party agrees to perform certain tasks.

## ENACTIVE AND PERFORMANCE MODES

Yet 'performance' is an aspect of marriage also. A popular usage provides a clue. There is an aspect to sexual intercourse which in some popular parlance is indeed termed 'performance' (similarly for both sexes?). And historically, as far as we know from general information, sexual intercourse is necessary for the 'consummation' of marriage. The absence of sexual intercourse can be terms for annullment and grounds for divorce. Assuming that marriage in the urban middle class ideology is still a relationship literally tied to 'law', we have the following situation: on the one hand, sexual intercourse may be construed as a sign of the existence of the code for conduct, as an enactment of it. On the other hand, there is something especially definitive about sexual intercourse, and the parties to it have acquired a relation that in a sense can never change entirely (*ex*-spouse, *ex*-lover); no longer is their relationship marked by the reserve of intimacy whose loss is signalled by the first act of intercourse.

Sexual intercourse does not bear the same relation to the code for conduct that feeding the cat bears to the code for conduct.

The diffuse code may be seen as an instantiation of 'law' or 'reason'. The legal act of marriage may be seen as an instantiation of 'law' or 'reason'. But there is a difference between the two.

In order to understand differences of this kind, let us suggest that there are two ways in which an action can relate to the relationship in terms of which the action is understood. One way we will call enactment; the other way we will call performance. Let us pose enactment as the relation between the diffuse code for conduct, and action 'in terms of' it. Particular actions relate to the diffuse code as enactments of it. As far as marriage is concerned, sundry actions may be seen as signs of the existence of the code for conduct. But at the same time, certain actions shade off into performance, which is associated with more specific standards for behavior (rather than more generalized diffuse codes), and the relation then begins to look more like a relation of contract.

The notion of enactment can be applied to the understanding of consanguineal kin relations. The unambiguous existence of natural substance (e.g., blood between parents and children) ideologically grounds diffuse codes for conduct (which is what acting 'as a parent' or 'as a child' means). These diffuse codes for conduct are realized through enactment (doing particular parental and filial things). The natural substance, the diffuse codes for conduct and the particular enactments can be seen in a sense as aspects of one another.

The existence of the code can itself be seen as a recognition of, sign of, implication of, the existence of a shared natural substance. Particular acts themselves become enactments of the code, whether or not the code relationship is seen to be as 'real' as natural substance is (e.g., the marriage relation may or may not be seen as creating one flesh and one blood, or some kind of spiritual unity).

We posit a close connection between substantialization, the existence of diffuse codes for conduct, and enactment, on the one hand; and between contractualization, the existence of more specific norms, and performance, on the other hand. However, the precise delineation of what is or is not substantialized is not given in the ideology itself. For example, people may find it plausible to believe that mothers instinctively know how to behave maternally—or that knowing how to behave maternally can be learned from a book one chooses to buy.

While any kin relationship potentially may be constructed by emphasizing more substantialized or more contractualized aspects, we feel that Schneider's analysis allows us to place marriage in a rather special position. And we can more fully appreciate Schneider's stress for the United States on the symbolic position of sexual intercourse vis-à-vis marriage, and vis-à-vis kinship in general through the native theories of procreation and relationships. For more paradigmatically than other relations, marriage among the people he writes about can appear to partake of aspects of both the world of substance and the world of contract. And one of the cultural reasons why this is so is because marriage (as sexual intercourse itself) in a more definitional sense combines both enactment and performance, creating the possibility of constructing the marriage relationship with an eye toward substance (ideas of spiritual union, the 'chemistry of romance') or toward contract and law.

A remark of Maine's is at this point worthy of repetition: "If any civil obligation bind together the Parent and the Child of full age, it is one to which only contract gives its legal validity" (Maine 1970 [1884] :164). At least under the capitalist mode of production, a social relation seems to need a basis, a footing, something which is its objective correlative. If a social relation just *is*, it may not be for long. The stamp of custom, or tradition, or even of volition, does not seem to be enough to guarantee it: it seems to need the stamp of contract and law, or the stamp of substance.

## PERSONAL AND ABSTRACTED DOMINATION

Schneider presents the cultural transformation of role theory: various culturally constructed definitions of kinship and other factors (e.g., age and sex) combine in the person. It is that combination which we ordinarily interpret as the norms of specific kinship relations. For example, if we consider the relation between parent and child: the kinship aspect is the aspect of substance and of enduring diffuse solidarity. The age aspect says something about biological age, and about relative skill and experience. The sex aspect says something about different characteristics attributed to differences between the sexes. The relative (or family member), as a particular category (e.g., 'mother') or as an individual, is a sort of sentence composed of these aspects.

However, since 'the family' is the paradigm for kinship in general, we may pose the following question: what are some of the general characteristics in terms of which the members of the family are differentiated? More particularly: what are some of the general characteristics in terms of which the members of the family are differentiated, which contrast with characteristics in terms of which people associated through contract are differentiated, at the same level of cultural definitions?

One of these ways has to do with the variety of social domination which applies in the family setting, at least in certain sectors of the population: domination of wife by husband, domination of children by parents. This is a sort of domination which we call "personal domination." In its simplest form, personal domination is domination not by some abstract entity (such as 'the market'), but it is domination by a particular person or persons of a particular person or persons. And it is domination not of something separable from the person (such as the person's property), but it is domination of the person as a person. (It should be clear that at this point we are talking of domination as reflected in ideology.)

The contrast would be something like "abstracted domination." In its simplest form, abstracted domination is domination of something separable from the person, by something separable from a person.[9]

The contrast is reminiscent of Weber's discussion of domination, and we may quote a now classic part of it:

> There are three pure types of legitimate domination. The validity of the claims to legitimacy may be based on:
> 1. Rational grounds—resting on a belief in the legality of enacted rules and the right of those elevated to authority under such rules to issue commands (legal authority).
> 2. Traditional grounds—resting on an established belief in the sanctity of immemorial traditions and the legitimacy of those exercising authority under them (traditional authority); or finally,
> 3. Charismatic grounds—resting on devotion to the exceptional sanctity, heroism or exemplary character of an individual person, and of the normative patterns or order revealed or ordained by him (charismatic authority).
>
> In the case of legal authority, obedience is owed to the legally established impersonal order. It extends to the persons excercising the authority of office under it by virtue of the formal legality of their commands and only within the scope of authority of the office. In the case of traditional authority, obedience is owed to the *person* of the chief who occupies the traditionally sanctioned position of authority and who is (within its sphere) bound by tradition. But here the obligation of obedience is a matter of personal loyalty within the area of accustomed obligations (Weber 1968: 215-216).

We would prefer to speak of domination directly, rather than to translate domination into kinds of authority.[10] We are including power and authority within the concept of domination.

One could actually draw up a four-fold table or a set of combinations. For an ideology which postulates a distinction between the person and things separable from the person: that which is dominated may be the person, or something separable from the person; that which dominates may be a person, or something separable from a person. The simplest combinations seem to be the least ambiguous: domination of a person by a person; domination of things separable from a person by things separable from a person. The complex combinations seem a little out of gear, even somewhat anomalous. For the purposes of this paper, "personal" and "abstracted" domination will refer to the simple combinations: domination by a particular person or persons of a particular person or persons; domination of something separable from the person by something separable from the person.

Note that we are not proposing that there is always a clear line between what is and what is not separable from the person. There is not necessarily a clear line. There is certainly not a uniformly agreed upon line. And the nature of the line, where it exists, is contingent on variable political-economic conditions. The qualifications do not detract from the analysis. The qualifications rather become its most important aspect, for the lack of clarity, agreement and continuity constitute problems which ideology attempts to solve. But that is a very complex argument. [11]

We return then, to Maine, even if we can challenge his ethnography:

All the forms of Status taken notice of in the Law of Persons were derived from, and to some extent are still coloured by, the powers and privileges anciently residing in the Family. If then we employ Status. . . to signify the personal conditions only, and avoid applying the term to such conditions as are the immediate or remote result of agreement, we may say that the movement of the progressive societies has hitherto been a movement *from Status to Contract* (Maine 1970 [1884]: 164-165, emphasis in the original).

But the return to Maine's argument is not absolute: instead of status, we posit the importance of the process of substantialization. That is to say: the contraposition of relations by substance and relations by contract (with the related action elements: enactment or performance) occurs as an historical development of the capitalist mode of production. And, at the same level, substantialized symbolism is the symbolism of personal domination, whereas contractualized symbolism is the symbolism of abstracted domination. Furthermore, contractualized relations in the narrower sense are inclusive of relations of class domination.

This claim constitutes an answer to a rather frequent criticism (made informally more than formally) of Schneider's work. It is sometimes said that his analysis at the "cultural level" is divorced from the realities of everyday life, is divorced from what real families out there in society actually do. Schneider has repeatedly made the point that this cultural level should be pursued as such as far as one can, before one attempts to find links to other aspects of social life. We might add: before the cultural level is embedded in other aspects of social life.

For here we find, full square, a point of embedding: of the world of symbols and meanings in the organization of the mode of production. We feel that our claim for this embedding is enhanced by extending the discussion of the relation between symbolism and domination beyond kinship and marketplace (or home and work) to religion and nationality, using Schneider's exposition (see section above).

As far as religion is concerned, Schneider admits he is rather recklessly passing over various sectarian differences, but a few points may be added, at least for Protestant Christianity: the idea of the soul, as internal to the individual in sense; the 'personal' commitment to Christ, in which one takes Him into one's heart and makes Him part of one's life. With a cleric as the medium or one's entire life as the medium, a relationship is made internal. Indeed, in the latter case especially, it is precisely the invitation to and from Christ to dominate one's life which seems to be at issue, a self-conscious joining of the Flock, for which the Blood of the Lamb has been spilled. One might say that part of the purification achieved by the Reformation involved the recognition of an inappropriate domination which qualified the domination of God.

In this light we should pursue the more substantialized elements (diffuse codes for conduct, enduring diffuse solidarity, love, loyalty, etc.) and their enactments more closely. The positive side of these things is a relation of trust, responsibility and mutual support, even togetherness, a relation of human being, partaking of a commonality which is, except to the grossest individualist and cynic, ennobling. [12]

But they have a negative side as well. Schneider writes of how, in kinship, the ". . .biological facts are transformed by the attribution of meaning into cultural constructs and they then constitute a model for *commitment* [emphasis in the original], for the passionate attachment which is one side of trust, and for the unreasoning and *unreasonable* [emphasis added] set of conditions which alone make 'solidarity' really solidary, and make it both enduring and diffuse" (D.M. Schneider 1968:117).

If one wanted to devise from scratch an idea which would legitimize total exploitation, it would be this sort of total commitment, in which almost anything goes, in which almost anything can be demanded.

The enduring diffuse solidarity of the nation is as much the death of Vietnamese and Americans as it is anything else. The enduring diffuse solidarity of 'religion' was at least as much the Crusades as it was anything else (see Hsu 1972). And the enduring diffuse solidarity of the family is still as much the domination of women as it is anything else: the domination of the labor and persons of women and their products (see Jensen MS.)

The relative diffuseness of the requirements of the relationships allows this sort of thing, which should itself be seen in a larger context. Consider the initial example of kinship. Diffuseness and enactment imply that the performance or nonperformance of a particular act is not taken as presumptive evidence of the termination or failure of the relationship. At the same time, diffuseness implies that the performance or nonperformance of a particular act is not taken as presumptive evidence of the success of the relationship. And while relationships of this sort may not be subject to precisely the same kind of calculus of success and failure as are contractual relationships, the ideology permits an easy slide into a more contractualized symbolism.

A diffuse definition of a relationship's requirements can have a liberating quality if the parties to the relationship participate equally in assessing the state of the relationship and its demands. But, however they may 'negotiate', if they do not participate equally in the negotiation, or if their specific definitions of appropriate action are for whatever reason conflicting, then the diffuseness of the relationship can function as an umbrella for domination, or for struggle, or for both.

Through this route we can see that if we are trying to understand the semantic features which distinguish 'parent' from 'child', 'husband' from 'wife', and so forth, we are not dealing with features which are somehow neutral parts of a cognitive system. Regarding them as such is itself part of the reproduction of the system of domination. The existence of such features must be taken as part of a system of domination and struggle. This brings up the next point.

The diffuseness of the requirements of relationships gives 'the family' (or other lower-order unit) a certain strength in the face of apparently external pressures. But that diffuseness also renders the family particularly vulnerable to those pressures. 'The family', of course, exists within a larger environment. One might say: the family is largely constituted by a larger environment, and largely exists for a larger environment. For most families, an essential part of that environment is a very particular necessity. In order to survive, members of most families must: (1) sell their labor power to a buyer of labor power; or (2) become a dependent of someone who does (see Eichler 1973, Jensen MS); or (3) in one way or another become a dependent of the State. People need not be motivated by a magnified consumerism or by a thirst for profit. They may merely be interested in maintaining a level of existence for themselves which treads a rather (in these days) uncertain water.

Insofar as the enactment of enduring diffuse solidarity requires money, and insofar as money can be obtained only through surrendering labor power, the scenario for the family's vulnerability to conditions apparently beyond it becomes more complete.

In an objective situation of inequality, then, diffuseness and domination are facets of the same social crystal.

Hence we can propose that the appearance of the domains (kinship, religion, nationality) as different, the specific similarities in their symbolic organization, and the structure of personal and abstracted domination, are aspects of the same totality.

The openness of diffuseness, as we have pointed out, provides a setting for domination. Everyday life, however, is not diffuse. There is some closure to the diffuseness. What are some of the ways in which it is achieved and legitimized?

## "CLOSURE" AND THE PROBLEM OF THE (LIBERAL) STATE

One of the ways in which closure is achieved and legitimized is through the utilization of inequalities which may appear to be internal to the unit. For example, 'within the family' the domination of women by men may provide such closure, the domination of the younger by the older may provide such closure. What is particularly interesting here is that the closure-providing inequalities are inequalities at least partially legitimized on the same substantial grounds as are given in the definition of 'the family' itself.[13] (Men, or adults, can be represented as authoritative because it is in 'their nature', and the family is a unit 'in nature'.)

Closure to diffuse definitions of relationships may also be provided by inequalities which appear to be external to the unit. The State is of critical importance, since closure may be achieved through the State's legal and bureaucratic apparatus which may determine whether or not spouses, or parents and children, are or are not fulfilling their diffuse obligations to one another. Among kin relations, the shading off from enactment to performance is not only a feature of marriage. For the relations between parent and child, the State can also stipulate certain sorts of action patterns as more explictly performing (prerequisite to the continuation of the social relation) than others. The legal apparatus may even determine whether or not substance itself is present or absent (as in paternity suits). And the State apparatus may legitimize its decisions in terms of its own substantializations: the general interest, the common good, the will of the people and so forth.

We might make the point more strongly as follows: diffuse definitions of the requirements of relationships exist in dialectical relation with the introduction of specificity into those relationships. This specificity may be introduced through a relation which appears to be a relation of a different sort, but which is either (1) itself a substantialized relation, with its own claims to diffuseness (e.g., male/female), or (2) a contractual relation with its own claim to another sort of necessity (e.g., employer/ employee).

Different emphases and degrees are possible within the same universe of relations: this is an insight which Schneider shares with Dumont. But which emphasis or possibility is realized at any one time is a product not of logic, but of real situations of domination and struggle, of the reproduction of a social formation, a point not stressed in Schneider or Dumont.

This point may help us understand why the symbolization of the 'nation' does not appear to be as tightly structured as is the symbolization of kinship. We would expect conflicts between and within classes to include conflicts over the identification of central symbols and meanings.

In liberal ideology, the State apparatuses (e.g., courts, agencies) are supposed to be instruments of the people, and their 'functions' include the guarantee of contractual relations. At the same time, State apparatuses can regulate the relation between performance and enactment, thus obtruding into units (e.g., chartered groups) and relationships (e.g., kinship) which, in the same ideology, are posed as being separate from those apparatuses.

At this point we may see some of the important differences which could emerge in a comparison between Schneider's American analysis as we have extended it, and analyses of other liberal (capitalist) democracies. A critical (but not exclusive) set of differentiating features would be those involving the "position of the State in capitalist societies" (currently a matter of much debate). Let us pursue this matter briefly:

One cannot create an "ideal type" of the American situation, even given the domination of American monopoly capital (Poulantzas 1974) and the export of aspects of American ideology. Symbolic forms in different liberal democracies are embedded in specific organizational features of other such societies, as well as in their position in the international division of capitalist labor and ownership (see, e.g., Grant 1970 [1965], Marchak 1975).

But we can still draw attention to the issue of the position of the State in general, and in particular to the forces (including competition between fractions of the capitalist class) which relate to the scope and nature of its intervention in domains which have the appearance of being separate from it. As was at least somewhat recognized as early as Tocqueville, the separation off of entities such as individuals and families, with a modicum of property to protect, can act to give freer play to large-scale interests as represented in corporations and governments, the actions of which powerfully affect 'individuals' and families'. Seen in relation to the tendency toward concentration and crisis built into the capitalist surplus accumulation process, the actions of such large organizations can increasingly appear to compromise both the opportunity to exercise freedom of contract, and the enactment of substantialized relations. The position of the State is critical in relation to concentration and crisis. At the same time as there are important differences in the relation of different States to concentration and crisis, one of the ideological problems faced by many of them is the legitimization, at different times, of increasing (visible) intervention and of decreasing (visible) intervention. It would be very unusual indeed—and not only from a marxist point of view—to encounter a situation in which the construction of a variety of categories (e.g., individual, family, nation, work) was not touched by this legitimation problem.

We might expect a more coherent general substantialization of the nation where the activities of the State, and people's relations to it, approximate the relations of personal domination. Such relations are quintessentially represented in times of crisis and the mobilization of the populace, aggressively, defensively, or both. Part of the very definition of 'normal conditions' may be that the power of the State apparatus is not exercised as an apparent personal domination over most people. But in the more aggressive and defensive moments, it is, through warfare and other sacrifices which people are called upon to make for the State.

THE INDIVIDUAL IN THE STRUCTURE OF SUBSTITUTION

But what of 'the individual'? With Schneider (and others), we may consider 'the person' or 'the individual' as the unit of action which articulates what seem to be different domains and characteristics. But the very condition of this structural position is that the individual is represented as a substance (see Mauss 1938): (1) concretely (the real individual individual, different from all other individuals), and (2) as Marx made so much of, abstractly (the individual as a faceless individual, equivalent to all other individuals).

Hence the individual is itself a substance as an individual, and individuals may also have substances internal to them which differentiate them from other individuals. Those differentiating substances can legitimize personal domination, as the notion of individuals as featureless substance can legitimize abstracted domination.

Assuming that Western logic operates: if an individual is to be dominated as an individual, that domination cannot be legitimized in terms of that person's uniqueness as an individual per se. This is so because ideology postulates that each individual is unique (concrete individualism). If an individual is to be dominated as an individual, that domination cannot be legitimized in terms of the person's being an individual in the same sense that other people are individuals (abstract individualism), because that sense undergirds abstracted domination, the world of contract.

The construction outlined provides a plausible solution. One might even go so far as to say that the construction is very intimately related to the provision of this solution. The plausible solution is to define the person in such a way that he or she is less than an individual in the contractual (performance) sense, an incomplete or unfinished or defective individual (see the quotations from Maine again). Since the individual is substantial, the lessness, incompleteness, unfinishedness or defectiveness itself becomes substantialized. Thus the legitimation of contract and of abstracted domination is preserved: individuals who are personally dominated are not individuals in the same sense as are other 'individuals'. [14] The presupposition of contractual relations is equivalent substance in persons (their 'common humanity'), and therefore a substance apart from the specific relations of the contract (a contract is, in the legal fiction, an agreement among equals). So while the individual is complete in order to be a party to a contract, that substantialized individuality is a prior condition and does not affect the particulars of the contract (the issue of parties to a contract falling under different jurisdictions will not be considered here). But this completeness is the empty completeness of equality, and so to dominate other persons directly, the ideology requires that the dominated person not be imaged as a complete self, not be imaged as fully human (Indians, Blacks, women, children, etc.).

This should not be taken as a 'lumping' strategy: we do not see Indians, Blacks, 'etc.', as instances of a unitary phenomenon called 'ethnicity'. Rather the implications for the construction of the self differ profoundly in each case. In the U.S.A., Black oppression poses the most acute problem, which we will briefly discuss later.

As Dumont points out, only after slavery, given the possibility of equivalence, did racism really develop elaborated arguments about the inherent inferiority of Blacks. The stress here should be on "elaborated" since the denial of fully human status to Blacks had to be initially discussed, especially by Jefferson, at the founding of an independent United States. [15]

The completeness and equivalence of persons in contractual relations is underscored by the legal 'fiction' of regarding corporations as persons. Corporations are indeed the perfect persons: complete, equal to each other, able to form bonds of various sorts, and powerful (able to actually apply their personness in the real world). [16] One might more accurately say that in the developing ideology, corporations are the metaphor for persons rather than the other way round.

Persons, corporate or otherwise, are most wholly individual in contractual relations. The premise of equivalent substance among such persons requires that personal domination be domination over something less than a person. To that extent, personal domination is transparent (behavioral and economic control is directly and immediately justified in the ideology), while abstracted domination is opaque (the ideology masks, rather than reveals, domination, here as the extraction of surplus-value, with the notion of equivalent selves freely agreeing to contractual arrangements in a free market place).

But we must bring back into the argument a point broached earlier. If one locates oneself within a more substantialized relation (e.g., kinship), and considers a more contractualized relation (e.g., employment) in contrast to it, the more contractualized relation appears as more external than, less real than, more accidental than, the more substantialized relation.

However, if one locates oneself within a more contractualized relation (e.g., employment), and considers a more substantialized relation (e.g., kinship) in contrast to it, the more substantialized relation appears as more external than, less real than, more accidental than, the more contractual relation (consider the felicitous native phrase, 'accidents of birth').

Considering the relations as a whole: that which appears as internal to the individual can appear as external to the individual.

That which appears as external to the individual can appear as internal to the individual. Phrased somewhat differently: that which appears as more accidental, more humanly constructed and less real, can appear as less accidental, less humanly constructed, and more real.

Since the boundary between personal domination and abstracted domination corresponds to the boundary between the individual and that which is external to the individual, a problem can arise. We suggest that the existence of this problem is not an artifact of our analysis, but is a real problem for those internal to this ideology, which (as we will see) emerges very clearly in the context of radical action. It is the double problem of alienation from oneself and alienation from others, a problem constituted by forms of domination.

If we take contractualized relations in general as given, we can question the necessity of behavioral requirements (e.g., behaving as a kinsman) as following from the existence of substance (e.g., sharing blood), without questioning the existence of substances, substances either internal to the individual, or of which the individual is part.

If we take substantialized relations in general as given, we can conceivably question the separation of performance from particular substance (made by contract), while at the same time not challenging the existence of the individual as substance.

The language of the substantialized individual and contract thus provides the meta-language for talking about both contractualized relations, and about relations such as kin relations which thus can be constituted as their opposite. [17] Could substantialized relations provide such a meta-language? One could propose that behavior in contractualized relations represents an enactment of individualism. But by doing this, one must stipulate the centrality of the individual, and one must allow for the substitutability of the two sorts of relations. These are all moves internal to capitalist ideology.

Hence the options within the system of relations provide a set of terms, structured in dominance, for their own description. This description reproduces the ideology up to the point at which 'the individual' is itself made problematic. But again, the ideology allows for this possibility by constituting the existence of the less than individual individual, who is dominated, and even the more than individual individual, who is dominating. The ideology appropriates its own paradoxes as part of the practice of domination.

## OPPOSITION AND THE STRUCTURE OF SUBSTITUTION

The theme of substitution must be carried further: it appears that in the United States at least, a variety of associations can be made between the concepts held by the dominating about Indians, children, women, Blacks. Psychological theories have been invoked to explain this occurrence. On what ground could it be possible for such symbolic substitutions to be made?

Lefebvre's concept of substitution (Lefebvre 1971) complements our argument so far. He argues that in advanced monopoly capitalism, commodity production establishes everyday life as a phenomenon of forced consumer choice. Images of action are subtly transformed into images of consumption, the fulfillment of which requires purchase. We may add that purchase is itself mystified as consumption. Everyday life has become the domain of the substitution of one element for another within limited universes of meaning (e.g., our supposed choices among toothpastes, cars, fashions, modes of leisure, etc.). Fashion style changes are a good example. These changes have little to do with function or with the body (neither of which change), but relate more to limited, self-completing configurations of symbols (e.g., the significance of one kind of skirt length derives primarily from its difference from another kind of skirt length).

In effect, once something is substantialized as the equivalent of something else, both participate in the same symbolic world. Here most importantly that world includes forms of oscillation from diffuseness to specificity, from enactment to performance and vice-versa. And so, if Blacks, Indians, whoever, are seen as partial persons (as being incomplete either inherently or developmentally), they can be located within the same domain. And this frames the forms of their struggle as follows: accept the domain and work with coalitions, or reject the domain and be isolated from mainstream discourse (as clearly seen in Black historical movements from integrationist to separatist and back). Ideologically, this prevents each from responding to the unique facts of their oppression, forcing them to choose among the same limited set of liberal options. Especially in the United States, it means that other groups innocently adopt prior forms of Black Struggle (e.g., Black nationalism preceded the Jewish Defense League and the 'Lesbian nation'). In American society, less-than-human status has been directly developed with regard to Blacks, and not in the same fashion for other groups (see M. R. Barnett 1975). This point underscores the significance of the study of instances of the apparent internationalization of forms of struggle (e.g., the import of aspects of the U.S. Black model by people in other countries). We should also be cautioned against the sort of international lumping which would reproduce in a still larger arena that lumping strategy of American ideology.

Three features, then, of this ideology:

(1) Relations of personal domination are substantialized;

(2) The ways in which they are substantialized tend to be consolidated so that they become similar in form (natural substance, diffuse behavioral definitions, the entire argument on homologous domains);

(3) The dominated elements tend to become symbolically substitutable.

Or: to the dominating, the world of negative substantialized relations can present itself as a unity of substitutable elements. Thus the ideology blurs the real differences between the real positions of different dominated groups. The ideology can deny the dominated the opportunity to authentically represent their own domination in their own terms (see Dolgin 1977, Magdoff and Dolgin 1977, Sartre 1965).

REVIEW: A UNIVERSAL OR A SPECIFIC STRUCTURE OF DOMINA-
TION AND SUBSTITUTION?

By this point, we hope it is clear that we regard the understanding of the form of a number of dilemmas to be impossible without an understanding of the same social whole. One of these dilemmas can be thought of as an intellectual or theoretical dilemma: "what is real?" Another dilemma can be thought of as a dilemma of action or practice: "how and with whom are we to act?" And a third dilemma is the very distinction between the first two: "is theory part of action, or apart from action?"

In order to understand the form of these dilemmas, the possibilities of substitution must be laid bare. These possibilities are in turn related to the forms of domination, which are themselves related to the kinds of representations which obtain of the relation between person and thing, between the individual and the social whole.

The notion of domination as used here refers specifically to domination within advanced capitalist society and is not meant to imply a "theory of domination in human society." We are talking about the ideological domination of individuals and this requires the prior ideological creation of antecedent, autonomous selves, a construction not present in pre-capitalist society. Given the individual, ideological domination is the forms of manipulation of selfhood which allow the reproduction of the capitalist social formation. Both the creation of the goal of 'self-realization', and the impossibility of reaching that goal because of bourgeois definitions of 'alienation', are the paradoxical forms of selfhood in advanced capitalism.

The construction of the individual (as empty substance leading to contractual performance, and as loaded substance leading to enactment) provides the path to self-realization and to the nature of obstacles along that path. Thus, to retain self-realization as a goal without questioning the construction of the self is as internal to advanced capitalist ideology as to say that alienation is given as the timeless, universal 'existential conditional of Man'. Internality to the ideology is basic here since self-realization is presented as a carrot on a stick (a possibility if only the 'system' worked correctly, a potent internal diversion in the U.S. since Watergate). Along with a notion of alienation as universal, this shifts the focus away from social movements to personal salvation as a return (if partial) to prior autonomy. [18] Of course, blocks to self-realization are an obvious starting point for a radical praxis. But unless quickly coupled with a critique of the self as part of the unity of determinations we are trying to outline, the starting point can become a crypto-bourgeois end (witness the recent movement of new left figures to a startling range of psycho-therapies). And here also is a crucial juncture for opening marxist theory, since Marx himself appears to have retained certain aspects of the individualist problematic while being acutely aware of the immediate implications of the bourgeois individual.

Domination as control (getting people to do what they 'must' do) is reflected in personal domination and abstracted domination. Personal domination (transformed from the pre-capitalist non-individualistic conjunction of enactment and performance and embedded in an individualistic ideology) characterizes the "incomplete" person and justifies control while retaining the concept of the individual (only some are more individual than others); equality among persons, the foundation of individualism, does not apply in this case and so is preserved. Abstracted domination expresses the form of equality within the ideology (empty substance creating its content through considered and 'free' choice) but can be seen as control from an external scientific perspective (that avoids the representation of the ideology to itself). Control or domination is evident in the necessity of choices ideologically given in contractual form. These are 'choices' only given the idea of empty substance and the possibility of self-realization through performance (either through work or the presentation of self as consumer). Otherwise, such performances are simply necessary to commodity production and consumption. Presenting them as choices allows the temporary condition of satisfaction and when satisfaction ebbs, provides the possibility of substitution (that toothpaste did not change your sex life; well, just try this other one!), given the taken-for-granted problematic of the individual. Theories of "rational" choice assume a construction of the self as the agent of choice.[19] Change these assumptions and the rationality of choice (the relation of choice to satisfaction) also changes.

While it may be easier to see the transparency of personal domination than to penetrate the opacity of abstracted domination, we suggest that these mutually shape each other. The use of domination in this essay applies to both forms, personal and abstracted, and sees ideological form given in the relation (as a structure-in-dominance) between the two.[20] This notion of domination starts from a critique of the taken-for-granted individual as antecedent to action, and is therefore meant to apply only to advanced capitalist social formations.

In order to get a sense of a contrasting possibility, we should consider S.A. Barnett's suggestion that in pre-capitalist states, one of the ways in which domination is legitimized is through the ideology of superior substance enjoining particular codes for conduct, and inferior substance enjoining particular codes for conduct. These codes include aspects of what we would consider contractualized relations. Pre-capitalist domination is thus transparent. It is not masked by ideology, even if ideology mystifies its source.

In pre-capitalist states, the problem of identifying equivalence and difference among persons does not have the same form as in our own. In pre-capitalist states the question of difference is in a sense solved. There are strata of differing substance and code. The idea of equivalence within a stratum carried with it not only equivalent substance, but also a ramified set of behavioral requisites.

The basic accommodation to capitalism (presented in India as colonialism) is the formulation of a personal substance which becomes separated from any social relations. Once substance inheres in simply Being, the possibility emerges for the kind of substitution, oscillation and double-binding which we have discussed. An act can be construed as occurring apart from one's nature. An act can be construed as reflecting one's nature. Precisely through this ambiguity, ideological control assumes greater importance in contemporary capitalist societies, since it can shift readily from substance to contract and back again.

The location of substance in the actor's essence rather than in the actor's actions allows that domination which appears as the outcome of agreement, the actor's performance being separated from the actor's essence, from the actor's nature as an individual. The location of substance in the actor's essence also allows for that domination which appears as the outcome of the actor's specific kind of essence, the actor's enactments being regarded as continuous with that essence.

These ideological moves are reflected in the homologies between domains which are ideologically separated (kinship, religion, nationality...), and link to the problem of identifying the equivalence and difference between persons which preoccupies capitalist ideology (including its anthropological variant). If we begin with the premise of individual equivalence in substance, how are we to account for differences? What is the ground of different action? Notions of empty equality despite differences (not the tautological equivalence of identities in the pre-capitalist sense), and notions of environmental causation (Locke's *tabula rasa*) are ideological rationales to cover the problem. Both distinguish performance from essence and make decisions about the relative importance and context of each.

The ideological separation of substance and performance, developed as work became wage labor producing exchange-value (that is, as work itself reflects new categories of being and doing), then structures the forms of domination which allow the reproduction of the capitalist social formation. (Diffuseness per se occurs since no criterion is determinate.) Homologous structures reflect the unresolved (and unresolvable) paradox that substance and performance, though distinct, can be substituted for each other (say in kinship, religion, nationality). The paradox appears as such rarely, if significantly, because the ideological claim is that these are genuine choices and that the oscillation represents real options given the 'best evidence' at the moment. [21] The definition of liberal discourse is discourse which always searches for this evidence, never challenging the structure of the options.

It should be clear that the two modes of domination can be substituted for each other in any domain. It is not surprising that the liberal response to awareness of personal domination in marriage is to draw up highly detailed marriage contracts ("I promise to keep strawberry jam in the fridge if you stay home four nights a week with the dog"). Or, in the other direction that recently Mayor Beame of New York asked city employees to voluntarily abrogate certain aspects of their contract so that we can all pull together and help our City in this time of crisis (enduring diffuse solidarity lives in the world of wage labor!).

These instances of substitution are not random; any substitution cannot occur at any time. A particular substitution occurs in the course of struggle around issues and acts to keep that struggle within the confines of the real as dictated ideologically. The movement back and forth between substance and performance appears as a real movement (as incremental progress) to those internal to an ideology since a shift seems to be won rather than granted. But as long as the distinction between substance and performance is perceived as part of the given (what an ideology places outside itself), the State controls the scope and significance of struggle since that distinction itself (not which mode is substituted for which at a given moment) is basic to the reproduction of advanced capitalist society. Substitution then is limited to those forms which do not challenge the fundamental construction of the person, a construction in which the State plays the decisive role.

Despite its intent, much radical activity is internal to the dominant ideology, to the extent to which it frames strategy around issues of substance or contract as if they bounded conceivable options, not seeing that struggle must begin with the recognition of the possibility of the oscillation between the two. On any social issue involving persons and groups, we can find a substance camp and a performance camp. (For example: the position that women should organize separately because of their different nature as women; the position that women should organize separately so as to achieve equality with men.) The separation of substance and action is thus linked to the possibility of what Marcuse has called "absorption." Even opposing views do not challenge the ideology at its root, but are accommodations with it.

From a perspective internal to the ideology, the significant question becomes the question of which view is 'objectively correct'. The apparent possibility of objectivity conceals a fallacy of misplaced concreteness. Since either view can become dominant in the course of struggle around a social issue, radical concreteness (as 'becoming') does not lie in one or the other, but in the form of their opposition (i.e., in the relation between them, not in either apart from the other).

## SUBSTITUTION AND THE DYNAMICS OF THE CAPITALIST
##   MODE OF PRODUCTION

We make the suggestion, then, that in the movement from status to contract... which means the progressive encroachment of contract... which means the enlarging of the sphere of class domination, the domination of the capitalist mode of production: that as this movement has occurred, the "remainder" is not an unorganized left-over, or a left-over still organized completely by principles which are in some sense survivals of an anterior mode of production. The ideology consolidates, recreates and reorganizes the non-contractualized in substantialized terms.[22] The ideology of individuals as equal, identical and separate monads itself functions to perpetuate and account for class inequalities, as Marx and Engels (see Marx and Engels 1970b [1848]), Marx (1970 [1852]), Sartre (1965), MacPherson (1964) and others have pointed out. Substantialization appears both as an accessory way of dealing with and perpetuating those inequalities (see Hsu 1972) and as a primary way of perpetuating and dealing with the inequalities of personal domination.

Aspects of the real internal contradictions of the capitalist mode of production, including the blocks to its expansion, can be represented by the ideology as obstacles which are external to the organization of production. While being represented as external to the organization of production, these obstacles can be represented as being internal to the person. Or, the person may be represented as being internal to them, thus alienating the dominated person from his or her own substance.

And the ideology can transform apparent external obstacles (e.g., socialist movements in other states) into the same set of relations as those which characterize the representation of the contradictions (thus socialism can be presented as if it *inevitably* involved a sort of personal domination), including the blocks to expansion. Since the development of the contradictions is uneven, since the relations between the specific forms of the contradictions shift (e.g., worker/capitalist vis-à-vis francophone/anglophone vis-à-vis material production/value production), and the relations between things proclaimed as external obstacles shifts (e.g., the appearance of 'severe climate' vis-à-vis 'high import prices' as explanations of high domestic prices) the specific forms of this alienation become somewhat elastic and elusive.

By blocks to expansion we refer to expansion in the sense of internal expansion (capitalist production relations overcoming other relations within the socioeconomic formation), and external expansion (other formations being incorporated into capitalist production relations). It thus becomes 'rational' to assume that elimination of the 'obstacles' (e.g., in a cruel paradox: of racism or of a race) can lead to elimination of the sensed aspects of the contradictions—to the elimination of failure, inflation, recession, warfare, poverty, etc. And it becomes rational to assume that elimination of the sensed aspects of the contradictions can lead to the elimination of the obstacles—to the elimination of racism, sexism, etc., on the one hand; of various forms of struggle on the other.

In reality, however: (1) one moment's obstacle is another moment's support (e.g., keeping women 'out of the labor force' may or may not be a 'good thing'; consider the notion that 'a woman's place is in the home' vs. the image of 'Rosie the Riveter' in the U.S. during World War II); (2) the elimination of the internal contradictions of the capitalist mode of production would constitute the elimination of the capitalist mode of production.

As action designed to overcome one obstacle (e.g., 'poor education') fails, another obstacle (e.g., 'lack of self-sufficiency in energy resources') may be chosen, with various sectors of capital winning out in either case. The ideology of rationality prepares the way for The Endless Search For The Real Obstacle, without recognizing itself as at least one real obstacle. Alternatively, one may move from the obstacles to the image of treating the problem directly (e.g., wage controls) and back again. Certain groups, however, are caught in the movement either way, and become doubly damned as both 'symptom' and 'disease'. The liberal and racist positions appear here most clearly as transformations of each other. The program of "eliminating the disease to eliminate the symptom" is the program of genocide. The program of "eliminating the symptom to eliminate the disease" is the program of the appropriation of authentic forms of struggle and culture. A movement between the racist and liberal positions is thus, tragically, a very simple movement, as we learn from Sartre (1965).

Thus the inequalities internal to capitalist contractual relations in the narrower sense, and the inequalities of personal domination, can be dealt with as if they were ultimately variations on the same theme, or less ultimately, as if they were explanations of each other (e.g., defective performance in the world of contract can be ascribed to defective substance; defective performance in the world of contract leads to personal domination). And the practice of each form of domination is part of the reproduction of its own conditions of existence, and of the conditions of existence of the other.

## THE CONSTRUCTION OF THE INDIVIDUAL FURTHER CONTEXTUALIZED

Given the analysis presented above, an everyday-life model of 'the individual' emerges in which the paradigmatic individual both dominates and is dominated: the individual as one kind of substantialization in an ideology that can, through substitution, substantialize anything. The individual as dominated by Higher Purposes substantialized through the State, Religion, etc. The individual as proprietor of his or her own substantial person, and of aspects of the substantial persons of others. The individual as proprietor of property, property which is both a precondition for and outcome of contract.

To return to Schneider: if we read 'individual' instead of 'person', the individual who is at the apparent center of the system is a fact and is a concept with a structure, a structure of domination. As proprietor of his or her own person, this individual must, as Schneider says, appear to keep certain substantial (irrational, natural, psychological, etc.) pressures down. This individual is also freed to keep down those who are imaged as being dominated by such pressures, which pressures allegedly prevent them from being full individuals. This picture supports our emphasis on the importance of understanding the corporation as person, since the corporation can be posed as having none of these (irrational, natural, psychological, etc.) impediments; it can image the perfect person. Indeed, as through substitution the metaphors are piled upon one another, we can have 'the corporate personality' and 'the corporate family'. Interestingly enough, such terms can refer to the 'individuals' who are 'members' of a corporation, or to subsidiaries which are owned by a larger corporate entity. These relations are relations which, in fact, are contractual ones, or which have their origin in purchase and sale. The use of personal language or family language presents the image of a nearly substantialized relation, an image which is linked precisely to the domination of owned by owner. From the "contractualization" and "commodification" of the personal and familial, we move to the "personalization" and "familization" of the contractual and commoditized. The image, however, remains an image, especially where 'management' retains the right to fire or to sell the members of its 'family', through procedures which (at least up to this point) are not exactly the same as the procedures for divorce.

Domination can appear to the dominating as able to confer the gift of individuality upon the less-than-individual, insofar as their less-than-individuality is reparable.

Consider Dumont's discussion of Locke:

... Locke's innovation stands crystal-clear before our eyes: subordination goes overboard, and with it the link it maintained between relationships among men and relations between men and inferior creatures: a split between the two is established, one would say is institutionalized: between men and non-men it is a matter of property or ownership: God has given the earth to the human species for appropriation—and homologously man is—in the second Treatise—God's workmanship and property. As for men, there is among them no inherent difference, no hierarchy: they are all free and equal in God's eyes, the more so as any difference in status would in this system tend to be coterminous with ownership [ Dumont's footnote 12: "... there cannot be supposed to be any such *Subordination* among us, that may Authorize us to destroy one another, as if we were made for another's uses, as the inferior ranks of Creatures are for ours" (II 6, lines 18-21)]. Let me add that as some kind of subordination is empirically necessary in political society, such subordination can be built only on the unanimous consent of the constituting members. Locke's law of nature pictures essentially a three-tiered world order: God, men, and inferior creatures, where equality characterises the human tier and where the relation between one superior and one inferior tier tends to be thought of as "property." This order is of course much simplified or impoverished as compared to the celestial and terrestial hierarchies of yore: it centres in the solidification and unification of the human species as against the rest of nature or terrestrial beings, i.e., in a man-versus-nature dualism which is warranted by the ultimate reference to the Creator (Dumont 1971:36).

We can present part of the achievement of the ideology as: (1) the substantialization of some inequalities, which denies the same individuality to the dominated as it affirms for the dominating, and which makes those inequalities substitutable in form;

(2) the apparent multiplication of ultimate references, or ruling forces, which may be substantialized as well: the Creator, Nature, the State, Mankind, Aggression, the Human Condition, Culture, the Profit Motive, the Facts of Life, whatever. The ultimate references themselves become substitutable insofar as their differences become irrelevant to the reproduction of the conditions of production. The domain of legitimate freedom thus becomes the domain of irrelevance, posing as the exercise of choice. Legitimate differences become (by definition) differences which do not make a difference to the reproduction of the conditions of production, although those differences may make a considerable difference to concrete people and their life situations.

The argument here may strike an unsympathetic note among those who try to live lives free of the domination of persons as persons, free of the domination of whatever it is that we and other persons regard as intrinsic to the person and inseparable from the person, should we agree on what that is. Such an attempt is not discounted by the analysis, but is rather highlighted by it. For this is an attempt to keep the ideology, and at least some of the proximate conditions which nurture it, at bay. But the argument also cautions that one does not break free of an ideology by a simple act of will, however well intentioned, that often one remains internal to the ideology through the very form of appearing to break free. One of the profound failings of the radical movement has been its tacit acceptance of the basic structures of ideological domination, rather than penetrating to the core of an ideology whose strength is shown in its ability to absorb radical strategies.

'The individual' in the taken-for-granted, everyday, common-sense ideology of the capitalist mode of production is thus neither a simple monad, nor the hierarchical and differentiated component of an organic totality. The individual appears, rather, as a relational monad: equivalent to other 'individuals' in general in dominating and in being dominated. Equivalent to other individuals in particular through a sharing of similar dominations. Different from other individuals in the specific content of that which dominates or that which is dominated. Different from less-than-individuals in achieving the proper balance of dominating and of dominated elements. This is a model of a kind of individual jostling for relative advantage. One can 'win' (dominate) in some situations, either as personal domination or as abstracted domination, and 'lose' in others. There is almost a balance-sheet that can be drawn up, reminding one of Lenin's phrase that a man can be a socialist in the factory and a tyrant at home.

This position of the individual in capitalist ideology partially grounds the terms of various approaches or schools of social science: we can and do see social action in terms of a broad-scale organization of society or culture; in terms of the nature and behavior of individuals; in terms of networks of relationship. For the individual as relational monad is, in John Fowles' phrase, "a walking oxymoron."

CONCLUSION

The concept of the person as relational monad, situated by the separation of substance and performance in an ideology of substitution, returns us to Marx's understanding of alienation (the break between persons and their life activity) as the transformation of a relation among persons to a relation among things (see Marx's famous discussion of "The Fetishism of Commodities and the Secret Thereof" in *Capital*, Vol. 1; Marx 1967 [1867]:71-83).[23] The idea of a thing for Marx is that which has an "objective character" (ibid.:72); that which is created by personal interaction (importantly as labor) but which stands as something apart and independent from that interaction. The alienation of commodity production is a product of the transition from feudalism to capitalism. In feudal society, "... there is no necessity for labour and its products to assume a fantastic form different from their reality" (ibid.: 77). Or, ideology in feudal society is transparent (i.e., it reflects the reality of feudal labor, not reality itself), while capitalist ideology is opaque (i.e., it masks that reality in "fantastic form"). This transition corresponds to the separation of substance and performance; prior to the emergence of capitalism, substance and action enjoined each other, being and doing were not separable categories. In such holistic societies, substance enjoining action structures relations among persons in all aspects of life.[24]

The transition to capitalism is marked by the distinction between use-value and exchange-value where value inheres in exchange (since to become a use-value a product must first be exchanged) and where the two are not directly related. "Could commodities themselves speak, they would say: Our use-value may be a thing that interests men. It is no part of us as objects. What, however, does belong to us is our value. Our natural intercourse as commodities proves it. In the eyes of each other we are nothing but exchange-values" (ibid.:83). And,

> ... the light from an object is perceived by us not as the subjective excitation of our optic nerve, but as the objective form of something outside the eye itself. But, in the act of seeing, there is at all events, an actual passage of light from one thing to another, from the external object to the eye. There is a physical relation between physical things. But it is different with commodities. There, the existence of the things qua commodities, and the value-relation between the products of labour which stamps them as commodities, have absolutely no connexion with their physical properties and with the material relations arising therefrom. There it is a definite social relation between men, that assumes, in their eyes, the fantastic form of a relation between things (ibid.:72).

This distinction between use-value and exchange-value in capitalism where "... value is realized only by exchange" (ibid.:83) corresponds to the distinction between substance and performance. Substance (and enactment) on the model of use-value is seen as given and directly stems from "physical properties." Contractual performance, on the other hand, has "absolutely no connexion," at least directly, with substance (although it ultimately depends on a prior individualist notion of substance). [25] Unalienated man, for Marx, is the totality of relations of both substance and action (expressed as the "unity between man and nature"; Ollman 1971:133). This is not meant in the Robinson Crusoe sense of a single individual interacting with raw nature, which would be an indication of a residue of bourgeois individualism, but rather to gloss a social formation where labor does not result in alienated products which then characterize social relations.

Alienation is first a separation from work, "... a break between the individual and his life activity" (ibid.:133). The implications of this break are a loss of control over the material world and over relations with other people (ibid.:134). Ideologically, the break between an individual and his or her life activity is expressed in the idea of individual substance not affected by or affecting contractual performance. The loss of control over the material world is also expressed by the separation of substance and performance. And the break in relations with other people is expressed through the tension between relations of substance-enactment, relations of contract-performance and the possibility of substituting one for the other. Personal domination or abstracted domination are the forms this last break takes either in terms of substance-enactment or contractual performance. [26]

Once the idea of the autonomous antecedent individual underlies an ideology, the two aspects of that individual (the substantialized and enacting, the contractualized and performing) are objectified, made into things and set on separate but interrelated courses. This is the initial movement in the transition from relations among persons to relations among persons seen on the model of relations among things. In the ideology under consideration, the substantialized and the contractualized are situated in an ideology of substitution where either form can be substituted for the other. Discussion of alienation can thus move beyond the discussion of a particular moment of substitution (as substance or contract, as enactment or performance) to analysis of the form of substitution itself. Or, action becomes problematic in a situation where the results of action continue the basic feature of alienation rather than restore and demystify the totality of social relations.

This raises the difficult matter of the relation between thought and action. There is a sense in which their disjunction forms the motif for our era and we are tentatively offering the direction of a resolution, a resolution which relates action to ideological form within a particular social whole, rather than relating action to elements of an ideology represented in such a manner that the social whole is backgrounded.

As with any analysis that seeks to understand historical form, we have had to travel a reverse path, first seeking to delineate that form as it is given to us, and reconstructing the genesis of that form (here as the problem Marx sets up in terms of a transition from relations among persons to a relation among things).

In outline, the path looked like this: first, we noted the centrality of the person; then, by seeing the placement of the person in various relationships (initially, those of 'kinship'), we could further analyze the person as participant in those relationships into a substantialized component and a contractualized component. We then indicated how the two components underlie two forms of domination, personal and abstracted, which emerge in the transition from feudal to capitalist production. And finally, we observed how these forms of domination occur as oscillations in an ideology of substitution.

# GENDER AND SEPARATIONS IN PRECOLONIAL BANABAN AND GILBERTESE SOCIETIES

The Banaban people during my field research were resident on Rabi Island in Fiji. Their home island is Banaba or Ocean Island in the Gilbert and Ellice Islands Colony, then a British Crown Colony in the Central Pacific. The Banabans were resettled in Fiji in 1945. I have discussed elsewhere aspects of Banaban culture in precolonial times and subsequently (Silverman 1971, 1972, 1977, 1978a, 1978b). Their current struggle as a people is to establish their rights vis-à-vis the mining of phosphate on Banaba, to secure a just and favorable constitutional position for Banaba, to secure control over their own future. What I am dealing with here may provide some ways of thinking about the intensity of that struggle.[1]

In this chapter, I engage in a great deal of speculation and I present relations based on information of very different kinds, and in which one has varying degrees of confidence. I use the best information now available to me about the Banaban people, I use information about the related Gilbertese to think out some of the gaps and to draw out some of the implications, and I use the Banaban ethnography to inform some aspects of the Gilbertese ethnography. The level of speculation is high, but not, I think, higher than that engaged in by others who are attempting to cast their analytic nets wide. The chapter is in part an experiment in the organization of some ethnographic data, an experiment directed by both the neomarxist problematic and what the available ethnography reports.

Our initial question is: how can one approach the question of production among these peoples?

*Approaching Production.* The production process is a process which unfolds over time, and through which people create time. In this process, certain people and conditions of production are separated from one another, and certain people and conditions of production are put into active relation with one another. The "relations of production" are those relations which both separate people from active relations with other people and conditions of production, and which put people into active relations with one another and with conditions of production.

For many Pacific Islands societies, gender relations (relations between men and men, women and women, men and women) are

relations of production. As soon as one begins to think of gender
relations as relations of production, however, an apparently curious problem emerges: some of the things which are being separated and unified are themselves aspects of gender (e.g., people's
sexuality, or something specific to one gender), while men and
women are the people engaging in the separations and unifications.

While gender relations structure separations and active relations
in the process of production, and aspects of gender are among
what is being separated and actively related, there is more than
that being separated and actively related. It is this which gives
gender the appearance of being both partial (one "principle"
among many, e.g., age, generation) and encompassing (once we
have said all there is to say about men and women, what else is
there?). What is being structured by gender relations is partially
but not totally reducible to gender. Gender relations separate and
unify aspects of men and women and also other things, that is,
things which are part of the same processes of production as
gender separations and unifications are, but things which are not
totally reducible to them. [2]

What are the non-reducible parts? In one way or another, for
many of these peoples the non-reducible parts have to do with
relations to the land and the sea. I am not suggesting that men and
women, land and sea, are *a priori* exhaustive categories, but that
both we and many of the peoples we study make these connections, and it is important to try and understand them.

They are not an arbitrary set. They are all *sources* of new
things, life-giving and death-giving things. And at least in the
Gilberts, they are not treated in the same way as other things are
treated. [3] On many islands in the Gilberts, people will offer things
to their relatives, things such as food, clothing and certain household items. Relatives may just take them from one another. There
are things which circulate rather freely among kin. But land does
not circulate freely. Large canoes do not. And people's sexuality
does not either (see Lambert 1963, Lundsgaarde 1966). At least as
far as land and women were concerned, people could get killed
for taking them away (cf. Lundsgaarde 1966:74, 108). "Reciprocity" starts, and stops, with these sources.

Men and women are sources and are the people who act in

relation to those sources (cf. Buchbinder and Rappaport 1976). It is this double fact which gives the analysis of gender some of its special difficulties, and which creates difficulties for the people themselves. The specific difficulties would not exist if the people did not separate certain aspects of men and women as sources, from certain aspects of men and women as the people who act in relation to sources. To understand those separations requires an understanding of the relations of production, which relations are also those which put what has been separated together as part of the continuity of the process of production.

An important thing about men, women, land and sea is that they are real. There are not only values on them, or commitments toward them, or beliefs about them. They are tangible realities. People who share relations through common substance, or some kind of land connection, share a reality with one another in social relationships. These social relationships are themselves realities, not fictions with the individual as prior. They are real as the people and their behavior and the land and the sea are real.

The nature of contemporary Oceanic ethnography directs our attention to these matters. What is interesting about some of the more recent ethnography is what analysts have found both difficult and exciting.[4] These things are largely about gender, as it occurs in descent, residence, politics, personality or pollution. I think this is in part because these topics represent what is in fact a single topic, a unity of "internally related" determinations (i.e., we regard the conditions of something's existence as part of what that something is rather than as "external" conditions; see Ollman 1971:28), which has been refracted through a variety of analytic categories.

*"Theorizing" Gender and Age.* One aspect of our problem is the theoretical conceptualization of gender (or "sex," in an older usage) and age in noncapitalist formations. Until recently, in many marxist (since Engels) and nonmarxist works dealing with non-capitalist formations, gender and age have often not been made problematic enough. The Women's Movement has taught us to be very cautious about the simple use of notions such as "division of labor" ("the sexual division of labor") and "role" ("sex roles") for these matters. The use of such ideas can mask real domination, and can suggest that what people do is separable from their

persons and their nature as persons in the same sense as occurs in capitalist formations. Marx and Engels suggest this in a number of places (e.g., Marx 1964 [1884] :109, Marx and Engels 1970a [1845-1846] :50), and nowhere more clearly than here:

> It is not the *unity* of living and active humanity with the natural, inorganic conditions of their metabolic exchange with nature, which requires explanation or is the result of a historic process, but rather the *separation* between these inorganic conditions of human existence and this active existence, a separation which is completely posited only in the relation of wage labour and capital (Marx 1973 [1857-1858] :489).

The theme of *separation* is one which we are taking very seriously (cf. Douglas 1966, 1970), and it bears on a subject necessarily raised in discussions of gender and age: the analysis of procreation and the relations in which it is embedded. The analysis of gender relations, including those having to do with procreation, should raise (and has raised) the analysis of separations.

In *The German Ideology*, Marx and Engels wrote: "The production of life, both in one's own labour and of fresh life in procreation, now appears as a double relationship: on the one hand as a natural, on the other hand as a social relationship" (Marx and Engels 1970a [1845-1846] :50). That the idea of looking at both procreation and work in terms of production was not lost is indicated by Engels' famous statement:

> According to the materialist conception, the determining factor in history is, in the last resort, the production and reproduction of immediate life. But this itself is of a twofold character. On the one hand, the production of the means of subsistence, of food, clothing, shelter and the tools requisite therefore; on the other, the production of human beings themselves, the propagation of the species. The social institutions under which men of a definite country live are conditioned by both kinds of production: by the stage of development of labour, on the one hand, and of the family, on the other (Engels 1970 [1884] :449).

We do not endorse an *a priori* distinction between two kinds of production, but look to what asking the question about such a relation tells us.

The gender and age issue, as we will see, is also illuminated by some of Marx's remarks made in other contexts. For example: "It is not the articles made, but how they are made, and by what instruments, that enables us to distinguish different economic epochs" (Marx 1967[1867]:180; footnote omitted).

And later in *Capital:*

The specific economic form, in which unpaid surplus-labour is pumped out of direct producers, determines the relationship of rulers and ruled, as it grows directly out of production itself and, in turn, reacts upon it as a determining element. Upon this, however, is founded the entire formation of the economic community which grows up out of the production relations themselves, thereby simultaneously its specific political form. It is always the direct relationship of the owners of the conditions of production to the direct producers—a relation always naturally corresponding to a definite stage in the development of the methods of labour and thereby its social productivity—which reveals the innermost secret, the hidden basis of the entire social structure, and with it the political form of the relation of sovereignty and dependence, in short, the corresponding specific form of the state. This does not prevent the same economic basis—the same from the standpoint of its main conditions—due to innumerable different empirical circumstances, natural environment, racial relations, external historical influences, etc., from showing infinite variations and gradations in appearance, which can be ascertained only by analysis of the empirically given circumstances (Marx 1967[1894]:791-792).

There is also a place, somewhere, where Marx calls attention to the necessity for understanding the control of people's time in order to understand essential features of social relations.

Relations between time, work, gender and matters anthropologists often deal with under the rubric of "kinship" appear in the following:

Let us now transport ourselves from Robinson's Island bathed in light to the European middle ages shrouded in darkness. Here, instead of the independent man, we find everyone dependent, serfs and lords, vassals and suzerains, laymen and clergy. Personal dependence here characterizes the social relations of production just as much as it does the other spheres of life organized on the basis of that production. But for the very reason that personal dependence forms the ground-work of society, there is no necessity for labour and its products to assume a fantastic form different from their reality. They take the shape, in the transactions of society, of services in kind and payments in kind. Here the particular and natural

form of labour, and not, as in a society based on production of commodities, its general abstract form is the immediate social form of labour.
Compulsory labour is just as properly measured by time, as commodity-
producing labour; but every serf knows that what he expends in the service of his lord, is a definite quantity of his own personal labour-power.
The tithe to be rendered to the priest is more matter of fact than his
blessing. No matter, then, what we may think of the parts played by
the different classes of people themselves in this society, the social relations between individuals in the performance of their labour, appear at
all events as their own mutual personal relations, and are not disguised
under the shape of social relations between the products of labour.

For an example of labour in common or directly associated labour,
we have no occasion to go back to that spontaneously developed form
which we find on the threshold of the history of all civilised races [foot-
note omitted]. We have one close at hand in the patriarchal industries of
a peasant family, that produces corn, cattle, yarn, linen, and clothing
for home use. These different articles are, as regards the family, so many
products of its labour, but as between themselves, they are not commodities. The different kinds of labour, such as tillage, cattle tending, spinning,
weaving and making clothes, which result in the various products, are in
themselves, and such as they are, direct social functions, because functions of the family, which, just as much as a society based on the production of the commodities, possesses a spontaneously developed system of
division of labour. The distribution of the work within the family, and
the regulation of the labour-time of the several members, depend as well
upon differences of age and sex as upon natural conditions varying with
the seasons. The labour-power of each individual, by its very nature, operates in this case merely as a definite portion of the whole labour-power of
the family, and therefore, the measure of the expenditure of individual
labour-power by its duration, appears here by its very nature as a social
character of their labour (Marx 1967[1867]:77-78).

I would like to emphasize Marx's observation that the different kinds of labor are "direct social functions, because functions
of the family," and that: "The labour-power of each individual,
by its very nature, operates in this case merely as a definite portion of the whole labour-power of the family, and therefore, the
measure of the expenditure of individual labour-power by its
duration, appears here by its very nature as a social character of
their labour."

These observations prepare us at least to entertain a possibility
of which there are indications in the precolonial ethnography of

the Gilbertese-speaking region: that these people operated with a "gender labor" theory of the evaluation of work activities, and what was considered socially necessary gender labor was in part a function of the requirements of the *reproduction* of the relations of production. I think the general point is made—if not in this language—in Geddes' recent study of Tabiteuea (Geddes 1975). As we will see, in the context of the foregoing, it is possible to use the idea of increment or "surplus" with regard to time and goods, and my discussion of it is meant to illuminate some of the changes which have occurred in the region since it was colonized, drawing leads from Salisbury (1962), Luomala (1965, 1974) and Godelier (1977).

One of the things that proves helpful in this regard is a way in which Marx conceptualized the "relations" between capitalist and laborer:

> The labour process, turned into the process by which the capitalist consumes labour-power, exhibits two characteristic phenomena. First, the labourer works under the control of the capitalist to whom his labour belongs: the capitalist taking good care that the work is done in a proper manner, and that the means of production are used with intelligence, so that there is no unnecessary waste of raw material, and no wear and tear of the implements beyond what is necessarily caused by the work.
>
> Secondly, the product is the property of the capitalist and not that of the labourer, its immediate producer (Marx 1967[1867]:184-185; see discussion in Balibar 1970).

I try to follow Marx's wariness about the uncritical export of notions developed for the analysis of capitalism, to the analysis of "precapitalist" formations. But my experience in trying to synthesize several ethnographies inclines me to think that Marx's point is a fruitful point of departure for theorizing certain aspects of the modes of production located in insular Oceania. Discussing the issue of "supervision" complements discussing the issue of "ownership," and in the Gilbertese-speaking area supervision is supervision of the activity or use of what people own (e.g., land) and what people produce (e.g., children).

*The Organization of the Chapter.* There are six substantive sections of this chapter. In the first section, I discuss some ways (mainly linguistic) in which gender is encoded in the Gilbertese-speaking area.

In the second section, I begin to discuss an idea of "gender productive capacities" and their use-values (keeping in mind Marx's observation—but being cautious of his use of "individual"—that "... where the economic aim is.... the production of use-values, i.e., the *reproduction of the individual* within the specific relation to the commune in which he is its basis...."; Marx 1973 [1857-1858] :489); related use-rights and the production of surplus.

I will use the term productive capacity very broadly. The ethnography of Melanesia provides precedents for the concept of productive capacity (see Burridge 1969), and also for using such a concept globally before making the kinds of incisions suggested by words such as kinship, economy, politics.[5] My analysis suggests that, seen in these terms, there may be fewer differences between the range of Melanesian societies and the range of Micronesian societies (Banabans and Gilbertese are classified as "Micronesian") than the terms Melanesian and Micronesian might imply. The focus also suggests a way of linking our understanding of at least some of the societies of insular Oceania to those of Australia (see Maddock 1972) and to the "hill tribes" of Southeast Asia (see Kirsch 1973).[6]

The third section opens the discussion of a few aspects of the organization of production through raising the problem of the supervision of production and cooperation in production, between men and men, women and women, and men and women.[7] The fourth section continues the discussion of aspects of the organization of production by pointing to concrete relations between men's and women's work and products in realizing use-value, and between evaluations of their activities.

In the fifth section, I begin a focus on reproduction and outline various aspects of reproduction and the capacity to procreate (invoking the incest taboo), to produce "materially," and to transmit rights in land. The section then moves from a description of the transmission of rights in land to a description of the transmission of rights to other heritable property associated with the Banaban bilateral descent system, including water-caves and ritual prerogatives. I address the question of how the exercise of productive capacity involved production for the producers and their dependents, replenishment for those who were producing for them or who had produced for them, and reproduction which involved an increment or "socialized surplus."[8] The work of Marx is of course important here, and also Lévi-Strauss (1969 [1949] ), Luomala (1965,1974), Sahlins (1958, 1972), Godelier (1977) and recent ethnographers of the region.

In the sixth section, I discuss some taboos (dealing with sexual relations in general, incest, menstruation and food) the violation of which was regarded as interrupting production (as I interpret the taboos), and which in some fashion involved the separation of the threatening people (in different ways) from production. I interpret the "threats" in the context of threats to the relations of production, and see their symbolization as constituting a theme of "counter-production" in dialectical relation with aspects of "production" discussed in the preceding sections.

I conclude with a few remarks on precolonial and early colonial Banaban history.

*Sources and Limitations.* In this study I draw on my own research with and about the Banaban people, seen in the light of ethnography conducted by Sir Arthur Grimble, H.C. Maude and H.E. Maude and more recent students, and also on material in Gilbertese dictionaries.[9]

Sir Arthur Grimble was a colonial officer in the Gilberts and on Banaba. His writings include ethnographic and ethnological papers. When I quote or summarize Grimble's statements and say that something occurred in "the general pattern," I refer to Grimble's general statements about the Gilberts which appear intended to apply to Banaba also.

For Banaba, I rely heavily on the first comprehensive description of Banaban society, published by H.C. Maude and H.E. Maude in 1932. H.E. Maude, the distinguished Pacific historian, was also a colonial officer in the Gilberts and on Banaba.

The well-known Gilbertese ethnography by H.E. Maude, Luomala, Lambert and Lundsgaarde has recently been supplemented by Geddes' volume in the series of reports from the Victoria University of Wellington Rural Socio-Economic Survey of the Gilbert and Ellice Islands (Geddes 1975). Geddes' data, which I also draw on extensively, are particularly important on matters associated with time and work.

Since my sources deal with different islands and different time periods, I tend to present some of their findings source by source. This gives parts of the paper the appearance of an annotated bibliography of quotations and paraphrases. I feel that my procedure is necessary so that the evidence for my assertions can be weighed most effectively. To this end I also try to "separate" the points being made into sub-points so that the interpretive liberties I take will be clear.

Given limitations of knowledge, time, space and research funds, I will have to gloss over many complex and critical matters, including details of the organization of production, and the development of "aristocratic" institutions in the Northern and Central Gilberts. [10] The absence of detailed discussion of such matters should not suggest their unimportance.

## SOME WAYS IN WHICH GENDER IS ENCODED

Banabans and Gilbertese acted upon the assumptions that men and women are different but they are both people; that men and women both have bodies, but they are different; that men and women have sexual-procreative organs, but they are different; that the differences in men's and women's productive capacities are linked to their bodily differences. We can look to the following for some of the evidence to warrant the foregoing conclusions: terms for men and women, gender titles, productive life-cycle terms, labels for body parts, and patterns of dress. The brief semantic discussion also leads to matters associated with marriage, land and trouble.

*Terms for Men and Women.* In Gilbertese, men and women are 'people'. One word means 'man, male'; another word means 'woman, female'. For the same gender, the same word is used as a noun (a 'man' or a 'woman') and as a modifier of a noun (a 'male' or a 'female' x). This feature can be interpreted as a linguistic one. But the 'man, male', 'woman, female' words are used in contexts where, in English, forms are used which are more specialized to the context. For example, 'the man's/male side' indicates the groom's family at marriage, and 'the woman's/female side' indicates the bride's family at marriage. The same pair of forms indicates relatives through the mother ('his woman's/female side'), and relatives through the father ('his man's/male side'). Where the descendants of a brother are being contrasted with the descendants of a sister, they are 'the descendants of the man' and 'the descendants of the woman' respectively. Gender is here being presented directly. [11]

*Gender Titles.* Before personal names, people can use a title meaning 'Mister' or a title meaning 'Ms.'. The male titles in use in the Southern Gilberts, and at times on Banaba, may be transformations of the definite/indefinite article. I think that Banabans tend to use the female title more often than the male title; women are somewhat "marked." [12]

*Productive Life-Cycle Terms.* There are some inconsistencies in the sources which give information on how people are classified as they progress, or as they do not progress, through the productive life-cycle. Some of the inconsistencies may reflect differences between different communities. But a few things are clear.

There are available terms at both ends which are genderless, for 'infants' and 'youths', and for the 'aged'. Nearly at both ends there are the rather parallel forms 'male youngster' and 'female youngster', and the parallel forms 'old man' and 'old woman'. For women, the 'young' part could carry meanings of both age and virginity. There is no real parallel term for men which accents virginity. When married, a woman became an 'adult married woman'. If she remained unmarried, she was 'the remainder of the generation', a term which at least these days often has the connotation of 'loose woman'.

For men, a 'male youngster' became an 'active adult male, member of the warrior generation, member of the fighting generation'. (In the Southern Gilberts today this is associated with marriage; see Lundsgaarde 1966:98). An unmarried man is a 'bachelor', and there is a report of a little used term for an old bachelor, 'remainder of the bachelors' (Sabatier 1954:637). [13]

In the middle of their productive life-cycle it seems that virginity and marriage mattered most for the definition of women, and vigor and perhaps marriage mattered most for the definition of men.

*Parts of the Body.* One source of insights into how men and women and their parts were differentiated is the manner in which the latter were labeled. Reconstruction here is fraught with particular difficulty because mission and government schools taught some physiology, and some of the usages may reflect that influence. I am using dictionaries as one of my sources, and the dictionaries themselves have a clerical origin. But we must do the best we can, at least to indicate the kinds of data pertinent to the questions being raised.

We can classify labels for body parts into those which are gender-specific (i.e., specific to the parts of one gender) and those which are not gender-specific. In Gilbertese, labels which are gender-specific refer to parts which have to do with sexuality and procreation in one way or another. Labels which are not gender-specific include some which have to do with sexuality and procreation, but they seem to be euphemisms.

Among the latter we find the common parallel pair: the man's 'badness, impurity', and the woman's 'badness, impurity'. The first applies to the penis, or more generally to 'male sexual parts'; the second applies to the vagina, or more generally to 'female sexual parts' (see Sabatier 1954:192).

A second term which is not gender-specific literally means 'the first boundary'. It is used for the transverse part of the abdomen under the navel, between the hips; another term indicates the part immediately above the sexual organs. The 'first boundary' term is also used for sexual parts, euphemistically and by allusion (ibid.:582).

Another term common between the sexes is a 'liquid, juice' term which is used for both male and female sexual secretions (Eastman 1948:215). [14]

We will now look at a few labels which are not the same for the two genders. Two such labels are the terms for the genders themselves: 'male' and 'female'. In their use for body parts, they may carry a connotation of 'the maleness of' and 'the femaleness of'. Some usages suggest a penis/vagina contrast. But according to Sabatier (ibid.:15, 514), the 'male' terms refers to 'masculine sexual parts', and the 'female' term refers to 'interior reproductive organs of the female'. This suggest both the unity of the notion of gender with sexuality and procreativeness, and a possible asymmetry, stressing the procreative side for women.[15]

These terms provide reasonable evidence that male and female sexual-procreative organs are politely represented as being of the

same order, but are at the same time differentiated from each
other and from other organs in the sense that other organs are
not gender-specific. [16]

The impurity theme surfaces again in a polite form for testicles
or 'male sexual parts' (Sabatier 1954:519), which also means
'detritus, garbage, impurity'. And in rude contexts, men at least
use a rather crude word meaning 'anus, backside' as an even
cruder word for 'vagina'.

As these organs are specially marked in relation to other organs,
so too are the forms of usage applying to them. [17]

*Clothing.* We can also look at clothing for markers of gender
differentiation. Two reports about Banaba from the nineteenth
century suggest that while men may have worn necklaces and
something over their shoulders, their genitalia were exposed.
Very young girls were naked, adopting skirts covering their genitalia (at least) some time around puberty or possibly at marriage.
Their genitalia were literally marked by being hidden as marriage
and procreation (and everything tied up with them) became possibilities or realities. [18] Another hint that women were specially
marked in this regard comes from what seems to be Grimble's
assumption, that "barrenness" was considered as a problem
afflicting women which a few old women on each island knew
how to remedy (Grimble 1921:32).

It is also useful to look at the labels for clothing.

One Gilbertese term for 'skirt' (of men or women) also means
'unpleasant'.

There is also a pair of terms, which have a kind of literal meaning of men's 'thing, property, affair', and women's 'thing, property, affair'. One of their senses is clothing: men's clothing,
women's clothing. Another of their senses is trouble: Bingham
glosses the male form as (1) 'a disturbance arising from the un-
faithfulness of the man', (2) 'stirred to anger or quarrel as a
woman in reference to a man', (3) (with a verbal suffix) 'to quarrel
with or assail a woman in reference to a man'. Bingham glosses
the female forms as (1) 'a disturbance with reference to a woman;
a woman-affair', (2) 'stirred to anger or quarrel with reference to
a woman', (3) (with a verbal suffix) 'to quarrel with or assail a
man in reference to a woman' (Bingham 1953[1908]:59). [19]

The female form also refers to a specific consequence of a

specific kind of trouble: it labels land given as compensation for adultery. On Banaba this land was known as 'the land of peace-making'. On Tamana Island in the Southern Gilberts, 'the woman's land' is a kind of dowry land which a parent has the option of giving to a daughter upon her first marriage if that marriage is one to which the parents consented (Lundsgaarde 1974).

I do not think it is too far-fetched to suggest a very close rela-tion among the following: maleness and femaleness; male and fe-male sexual-procreative organs; male and female clothing; dis-turbances provoked by the (sexual?) misbehavior of one gender vis-à-vis (always?) a member of the other gender; and land, as compensation for adultery (a 'woman's affair') and as the land which a woman may bring to her marriage. [20]

### GENDER, USE-VALUE AND USE-RIGHT

Seen as territorial units, five village districts constituted Banaba. [21] The village districts were composed of hamlets, and the hamlets were composed of households. Generally, a house-hold family owned a canoe shed on one of the coastal terraces and in the household compound had a sleeping house, a cooking and storage shed and a small 'house of menstruation' for men-struating women family members (Maude and Maude 1932: 269). Some hamlets apparently did not have a 'house of menstru-ation', but used a special part of another house for menstruating women. [22]

The household thus had a place for men and for women (the sleeping house), a place in which most of the work was done by women (in the general pattern, women cook), a place for women when they were not working (the 'house of menstruation', or part of another house) and a place for men (the canoe shed, fishing beyond the reef being a male activity). Men did things on the sea; men and women did things on the land. On Banaba women also did things under the land: only they could enter the underground water caves which (especially in times of drought) were indis-pensible to life.

On Banaba, for everyday production purposes, people probably associated with one another on gender and household-cum-net-work lines. In what was a small population (probably between five

hundred and one thousand), the available technology for dealing
with fish, tree products, wells and water-caves presented itself
as one permitting a variety of lines along which subsistence could
be concretely organized.

With some variations of detail from island to island, in Gilbertese-speaking communities there were general differences
between men's and women's work, even when men and women
were working together in the same productive activity (see Luomala 1974 on swamp taro). Men fished in the deep sea (and did
things related to fishing and navigation), acquired fish close to
shore, supervised many things, engaged in war and tasks requiring
'strength' (such as carrying heavy burdens), cut toddy and climbed
trees for other purposes, cultivated (in the Gilberts), participated
in ritual games with frigate birds. Fishing was extremely important; even today, your catch is called 'your capability' (which
may also be glossed as 'your conquest'). On Banaba in particular,
men performed the *kouti* ritual, about which, unfortunately, I
know little. This was a ritual men performed on the coastal
terraces to ensure their "success and prowess," while they were
facing the rising sun, which was the source of "health and
strength" (Maude and Maude 1932:281).

Women participated in cultivation (in the Gilberts), acquired
fish close to shore, obtained water, prepared and served food,
made mats, sennit, and coconut oil, boiled toddy, fished from the
reef, looked after young children and had important responsibilities at critical moments in the productive life-cycle.

The men's and women's activities mentioned include those
which were stressed in what we may term the formal education
of young Banabans and Gilbertese, as indicated through rites of
passage. And what for our purpose is the most interesting thing
about formal education is that it was primarily in the hands of
people of the same gender. To a significant degree, men developed
the productive capacities of men and women developed the productive capacities of women. Men acted on the world in similar
ways, often in the company of other men; women acted on the
world in similar ways, even more often (as we will see) in the
company of other members of the same gender.

The different capacities of each gender can also be viewed as
the different "properties" of each gender, since members of one

gender were positively forbidden from doing things reserved by the other (for an example, see Lambert 1963:162).

I hope the rest of this chapter will demonstrate that we can introduce a fair coherence into the ethnography of the region by assuming a productive capacity tied to gender, and also by assuming that that capacity took three forms which were treated differently yet were linked within production and reproduction. They differed in that for many purposes their use-values were different. To label the differences I use the terms procreative, "material," and the transmission of property. [23] Generally speaking, men and women (if not in the same ways) had the capacity to procreate children, who could further procreate children and thus preserve or replenish what was transmitted to them or expended for them, and who could reproduce. Men and women had the capacity to produce "materially," meeting their own consumption needs and those of their dependents (especially their children); the consumption needs of those who were producing for them or had produced for them in everyday life (especially parents and grandparents), thus "replenishing" the latter; and furthermore producing a surplus to be "socialized" in reproduction. Men and women had the capacity to transmit heritable property, in such a fashion that further heritable property could be transmitted. Men and women had to do these things within (social) relationships, which were defined in terms of them.

As people dealt with one another in a variety of contexts the existence of these capacities was recognized, and the exercise of one (e.g., procreation) had implications for the exercise of another (e.g., the transmission of property). That these three were a linked yet not undivided unity can be established on cultural grounds. Here the treatment of sexuality (which was tied to procreation) is critical. Engaging in sexual intercourse was separated from other productive activities (see below) and, generally speaking, spouses did not transmit property to each other but to their children. That the transmission of property was separated from the others is indicated by the "ritual" aspects of the descent system, in the activities of which affines (as affines) did not participate, while on the other hand affines could cooperate in material production and participate in some kindred activities. [24]

This argument has been informed in general by Sahlins 1972

(chapter 4), Godelier 1977 (chapters 4, 5 and 9), and more specifically by Luomala, who writes about the Gilberts but in the context of a general Oceanic pattern in which, on an island, "... one or two plants may provide vegetable foods, and a different plant provide the festive food" (Luomala 1974:16). The "festive food" in the Gilberts (*Cyrtosperma* or "swamp taro") is involved in clear ownership patterns, the emphasis is on the work of one gender, and there is "attempted overproduction" (in Luomala's phrase) to demonstrate skill and to contribute on social occasions, giving prestige (see also Luomala 1965, in which surplus is discussed directly).

The differentiation of aspects of productive capacity which I suggest the people made relates to three kinds of use-rights which are also linked in the process of production and reproduction: use-rights in material productive capacity, use-rights in sexual-procreative capacity, and use-rights in heritable property, including land, water-caves and ritual prerogatives.

These relations are suggested in the language itself. The semantics of a number of Gilbertese categories indicate that there is a very close link between ideas, as there is between practices, of using things (and when people exercise productive capacity they are using things), exercising use-rights toward things, and holding use-rights over things, which are ways of 'actively relating toward' things (and ways of talking about relations with kin and affines are rather similar to the foregoing). These ideas and practices are in turn internally linked to 'inheritance' (or in another gloss, 'transmission'), which is a state into which people are put by others. Indeed, the most general term for 'thing' is also the most general term for 'property' (Silverman 1978b). [25]

But rather than get lost in things, we will continue the discussion by raising the question of how, in production, gender was relevant to cooperation and the supervision of the ways in which people 'actively related toward' that which they actively related toward.

FROM THE POINT OF VIEW OF PRODUCTION:
SUPERVISION AND COOPERATION

*By Men, With Men.* We will begin with older accounts about
Banaba and the Gilberts, and then introduce data from a more
recent account.

On Banaba, the son lived with his parents until the time of his
male initiation, which occurred "... soon after the appearance of
his axillary and pectoral hairs" (Maude and Maude 1932:68).
Between the beginning of the initiation and his assumption of
the status of 'active adult male' (more narrowly translatable as
'warrior', or 'of the war generation', or 'of the fighting generation'), ready for marriage, he spent a good deal of his time in the
'young men's house' (also translatable as 'bachelors' house'), or
on the coastal terraces. During this time, elder men instructed
the boys in family traditions and in the *kouti.* Men built platforms
near the terraces for their performance of the *kouti.* The *kouti*
performer could not go near a woman or sleep on a mat on which
she slept, so the performer would live on the terrace before doing
the ritual. [26]

The Gilbertese boy may have been removed when younger.
According to  Grimble, until about five years of age the boy interacted with women in his daily life, as he was not yet 'reasonable'.
Before his fifth year, during his first hair-cutting ceremony, two
charms were recited "... to protect him from the wiles of the other
sex, for all communication with women before ritual should have
made him fit for marriage was considered liable to make a coward
of him" (Grimble 1921:37). At five years of age, the boy's father
performed a ritual which indicated that the boy was no longer an
infant. After that he could sleep only beside males, and was in
many ways separated from women (ibid.).

In the Gilberts, at about ten years old the boy probably went
to live with his father's father or father's father's brother, who
became his guardian. [27] The boy took the elder's name. The boy
cared for the elder, as his own father was too busy with other
work to give the required attention. The elder taught the boy
Gilbertese history, genealogy and science, and rewarded the boy
for his care with a large piece of land which the boy could transmit to his own children. This relation between  guardian  grand-

father and grandson "... had some curious results, not the least strange of which was the decay of the local genealogies, for as these have been handed down from grandparent to grandchild since very early days, alternate generations have often been skipped...." (Grimble 1921:38).

This grandfather had a special role in activities to which we will allude shortly. Grimble's brief comparative description of what occurred on Banaba makes less of the grandfather's role. But boys were instructed in the *kouti* ritual by a grandfather or other senior relative (Maude and Maude 1932:268, 283).

In the general pattern, according to Grimble, when approaching the age of betrothal, the boy's diet was restricted and he engaged in hard work in order to impress potential parents-in-law. Here the boy began a series of ordeals supervised by male kin when his pectoral and axillary hair grew. At a particular time in this sequence of activities, he was sequestered in a small hut for a considerable period, out of contact with women. Elders brought him his food, and his grandfather "set him tasks of strength, hardihood and endurance to perform." He was supposed to "... think only of deeds of strength, the day's task, the valour of his forebears, and all things befitting a worker and a warrior" (Grimble 1921:40). After more activities he became an 'active adult male, warrior', and was often soon married. [28]

This reconstruction of precolonial patterns is complemented and deepend by Geddes' recent description from North Tabiteuea in the Southern Gilberts (Geddes 1975). Geddes describes the work patterns and relations of people of different gender and age in the Gilbertese *mwenga* 'household', a unit the importance of which was upgraded by the colonial administration. The organization of the household today thus cannot faithfully reflect its organization in the past. However, what Geddes describes can be so neatly tied to the older accounts that I will take the risk of assuming a broad continuity.

According to Geddes, young children are not allotted specific tasks although they do accompany older people as the latter work, and imitate their activities. Until four years of age, children are "... placed under the care of older persons in the *mwenga* who are responsible for keeping an eye on them at all times. Children of this age are therefore one of the recognized reponsibilities of the

*mwenga.* During the day one person may care for the children of
several *mwenga* where the women work together" (Geddes 1975:
35).

Between seven and eleven years of age children generally
attend school and perform 'light' chores requiring little skill. [29]
These chores include looking after younger children, and productive activities including the acquisition of fruit (during which children are usually accompanied by older household members), shellfish (usually done by older girls), stranded fish (accompanying
women), pig-feeding, toddy-cutting (boys accompanying men), and
torch fishing in the lagoon (children "... help older women to
gather dead coconut fronds and tie them together to form long
thick wads" before torch fishing; ibid.:36).

Between twelve and eighteen years of age, boys accompany
elder men in toddy-cutting, learn the process from them, and then
can cut toddy on their own. They also learn taro cultivation,
engage in net fishing, and collect fruit—in the latter task often
being accompanied by still younger children. Occasionally boys
will accompany men on canoe fishing. Older people "tolerate"
children of this age, but do not really include them in their discussions and activities (ibid.:38).

Between nineteen and thirty years of age, males

> ... take more responsibility for the day to day running of a *mwenga.*
> They spend less time in the activities of youths and more time in the
> company of older men. They are now accepted in the older men's groups
> and progressively allowed to express opinions on topics under discussion.
> Initially these opinions are likely to be an echo of older men's statements.
> An older man will look to a younger man to support him in a discussion
> and may often refer to the young man for that support. By the age of
> 30 years most men are expressing their own opinions and taking an active
> part in discussion (ibid.:39).

A younger man, probably now married, learns skills relevant to
his new position and family, in "... fishing, canoe building and
repair, house building and repair and work on his lands" (ibid.:
39). The young man goes on fishing trips with older men, and
works in housebuilding for kin.

By this point men have learned requisite skills, but not

... the 'law' underlying the traditional skills they have been taught by older relatives. This 'law' is taught at a much later time, usually at the death-bed of the relative and only to the few relatives specially selected to be taught it. They are however skilful in the practical execution of the skills they have learnt (ibid.).

Older kin have supervised them until they have mastered the skills.

Most men necessarily set up house near their own kin when first married. This is required since a man will learn skills necessary to the running of a *mwenga* from his own kin but not from the kin of his wife. The most important of these skills are not learnt until marriage and it is not possible for a young married man to decide that he will move away from his own kin unless he is willing to forfeit his right to learn those skills (ibid.).

Between thirty-one and fifty-nine years of age, men are in a position to have younger members of their family do chores which the former had performed themselves, and thus to engage their skills in fishing, cultivation, etc.

*Mwenga* headed by men in this age group tend to become increasingly independent of older kin and other *mwenga* though the house site is still close to those of other kin. The man is now entering the period in life where he will take up the role of instructor rather than the instructed and he is therefore far less dependent on others (ibid.:40-41).

Beyond sixty years of age, men become more dependent on younger kin for food and other things, advise rather than participate in household productive activities, and are treated with "deference and respect." Elders teach the 'law' of special skills to relatives who have been solicitous of them. Old men spend time talking with others and caring for small children, as younger people work; old men also rest in the 'meeting house' and at home, becoming less mobile and thus working less outside the household.

The picture for Banaba would have been somewhat different. On North Tabiteuea: "Ties between the husband's kin group and the *mwenga* are very much stronger than those between the household and the wife's group" (ibid.:25). This was reflected somewhat in who was living with whom. Banabans speak more in terms of a special obligation of the son-in-law to the wife's parents, especially the wife's father, which could have involved the couple's living with the wife's parents. One way people explain this is as follows: Both sons and daughters had 'debts' to their parents, for what the parents had expended in bringing them up. The son had already 'untied' that debt somewhat, through the difficult tasks in which he engaged while growing up, although he still had obligations to both parents. The daughter had to find a man to untie her debt, to produce for her, for her father.

In one sense: poor men. Lucky women! And this is one of the ways in which people talk about the situation. At times they contrast it to the Gilberts, where the woman rather than the man is the drawn-in 'worker'.

From both the older and more recent accounts a general picture emerges which we can draw as follows: The appearance of a specifically male productive capacity should be understood in the context of relations both within and between genders. The difference between the "material" and procreative use-values of that productive capacity should also be seen in that context. This is for (at least) two interrelated reasons. First, sexual relations are between genders, not within them. Second, in the old days, older men supervised the separation of boys from women, and the subsequent bestowal of use-rights in the procreative capacity of men (this will be elaborated in a later section).

I want to draw attention to the question of supervision (also mentioned in Lundsgaarde 1966; see also Lambert 1963, Silverman 1971). The two accounts I am using suggest that older men supervise the work of younger men, as older men not only teach skills to younger men, but also transmit knowledge to younger men which is the elders' property. As men age and marry they begin supervising the work of males who are younger still. As the process develops, the younger men engage in work which the older men had previously conducted, thus freeing time for the elder men to engage in more specialized subsistence activities and, in precolonial times, ritual and perhaps warfare. The male "movement through the life cycle" may have been interpreted culturally as a movement from activities requiring less skill ("less specialized") to activities requiring more skill (the latter including some "subsistence" activities as well as warfare and ritual) and *further time* to develop (cf. Lambert 1963:251-252).

Geddes makes the general point that:

The more important the resource or product of a resource is in the community the more rigidly are the production possibilities controlled and the more complex the skills involved in its utilisation. To attempt to utilise such a resource or product outside of the socially acceptable ways causes a social reaction against the offender who is thus brought back into line. For these reasons a great deal of time spent in the production of certain economic goods is not strictly essential to production but is essential if the product is to be socially approved (Geddes 1975:54).

Elder men's supervision of how younger men produce shifts to elder men's use-rights in the products of the youngers' productive capacity which, as kin, the elder men have. (For the Banabans, at least, the father-in-law had a special use-right of this kind.) The shift from supervision of work to claim on product (and time) in a general sense coincides with the shift from an emphasis on less skilled to an emphasis on more highly skilled activity. Both occur as elder men transmit property to younger men, as the work of younger men gives elder men further time to engage in the latter's more highly specialized activity.

"Subsistence activity," however, may have appeared as being somewhat distinct from "ritual activity" in that older men may have continued in this ritual activity in a way in which they did not continue in "subsistence" activity. At the same time, subsistence and ritual activity could appear as aspects of the same basic operation—because they were, in the relations between men, and the sites of some of the most important subsistence activity (fishing) and ritual activity (the *kouti*) were linked in being on the coast. If the same pattern applied on Banaba as in the Gilberts, the sanction of the leader of the meeting-house was such that violators of his judgments could become 'accursed', and his sacred amulet, associated with his cursing power, was "... made of a single coconut leaflet which had grown 'facing the sunrise on the eastern shore of the island' " (Maude 1963:46).

*By Women, With Women.* Let us again begin with the older accounts and then bring in the more recent one. We will encounter many of the same points that we encountered in the last section, while at the same time discovering differences between the situation among women and the situation among men.

On Banaba, the daughter lived with her parents at least until her marriage, which usually occurred soon after puberty.

Grimble discusses a first menstruation rite, during which the girl's body was anointed with coconut oil day and night. The oil was applied by her guardian grandmother. [30] This grandmother supervised the recitation of "charms" which "... were nearly all directed towards parts of the girl's body with the object of increasing her beauty and making her a mother of men" (Grimble 1921:42). (Banabans stressed procreating both sons and daughters.)

The guardian grandmother then took the girl to a fresh water well where she bathed while the grandmother recited a spell, 'the washing of blood'. [31]

Many contemporary Banabans celebrate a kinswoman's first menstruation. While both men and women are present during the activities, the girl in question stays in a separate room watched over by elder women, and engaging in women's activities such as mat making, until the last day, when she joins the feasters.

First menstruation is an event to celebrate, while the menstruation is itself unclean and negative. (It is said of a menstruating woman that 'she bleeds', or 'she is sick'. A common name for the first menstruation event is 'the sickness'.) [32]

At the time of marriage, in the general pattern, the groom's relatives built a house for the new couple. The bride's mother, mother's sister, mother's mother, or adoptive mother brought her into the house. Then the boy was brought in by his mother or father's sister. He went to the bride encouraged by his close female kin. The bride's virginity, or lack of it, was attested by the groom's mother, who entered the house and searched for traces of blood on the sleeping mat. Grimble describes a practice for Banaba which sounds rather implausible, but the point being made was very plausible: The same virginity test existed as in the Gilberts, but the young couple were sequestered in a hut until the bride was pregnant, or was known to be barren (Grimble 1921:32). Contemporary Banabans comment that if a girl were found not to be a virgin upon marriage, her whole family would be shamed. Her mother would bear a particular shame as the event would mean that she had not correctly looked after her daughter. In representing the "interests" of her own family, the groom's mother was also implicitly evaluating the mode of upbringing guided by the bride's mother.

According to Grimble's general description for the Gilberts, when it was known that a woman was pregnant, she "lay apart from her husband," under the care of her mother or other female kin, who stayed with her for the duration. Grimble observes that the husband's female kin were often considered more reliable as chaperones of the wife than her own kin were. During the last three months of pregnancy, two of the mother's kinswomen, or friends if skilled kinswomen were unavailable, came to confine the expectant mother, to help with the pregnancy and birth.

Geddes writes as follows about girls between twelve and eighteen years of age on North Tabiteuea today: "Most of the activities of girls in this group are done in the company of older women who supervise and instruct them" (Geddes 1975:36). These girls clean the house and house site, care for younger children while older women do other things, perhaps looking ". . . after the small children of several neighbouring *mwenga* freeing women from these houses to work together" (ibid.). The girls help older women in preserving pandanus fruit, they learn how to make some articles from coconut fronds and pandanus; they acquire shellfish, usually with younger children. They can accompany boys in netting fish. "All a young girl's work is closely supervised and older women speak scathingly of *mwenga* where young girls of this age group are expected to do a woman's work without supervision" (ibid.). It is important to observe, as Geddes does, that these girls have been defined as 'women' in the puberty ritual but are still not responsible for directing their own work. It is also interesting to observe that boys do not have a puberty ceremony at this time—but that a boy of the same age as the girl will eat with her at her puberty ceremony, marking a difference between older and younger boys; the girl's puberty ceremony is being used as a way of marking the puberty of both girls and boys.

Recall that boys of this age cadre do not yet regularly accompany men in canoe fishing. By contrast, girls are already involved in the range of female subsistence activities, although their skills are not regarded as being fully developed. After puberty, girls are also not as "free-ranging" as they used to be; when they travel they need escorts, and they cannot "... form close friendships with members of the opposite sex" (ibid.:37). Boys of equivalent age are freer to move about, but girls, as boys, do not participate actively in adult discussions.

> Many of the activities of this group are designed to free older women of the *mwenga* for more specialized activity and older women will leave most of the routine work of an activity to these girls. The amount of work done by a young girl is directly dependent on the number of older women in the *mwenga*. Where there are several older women the girl will be required to do less around the house and will spend more time in straight-forward nursing of babies and young children. Where there is only one older woman the girls are expected to do a great deal more work around the home" (ibid.:37).

Between nineteen and thirty years of age, women take more work responsibility and have usually been married. Even if living with their husbands, they are "... likely to be under the direct influence of at least one older relative and usually several older relatives from neighbouring *mwenga* who do their chores together and expect the young women to join them and accept advice and direction from them" (ibid.:38). The husband's kin should teach her the household skills she does not yet know (which are several) and improve her performance of what she knows already. Thus, as far as various "subsistence" activities are concerned, the woman at marriage moves (to a degree) from the supervision of her own female kin to the supervision of her husband's female kin, while the husband is still learning from his male kin for a time after marriage.

Between seventeen and twenty-five years of age, unmarried women visit relatives in other villages, and enjoy a larger measure of freedom of movement while away from home. At home, women do a good deal of work—"domestic" in the sense that they are, for example, growing food for members of the household, but not "domestic" in the Western ideological sense of engaging in activities within the confines of the house.

Until she has children the woman is

> ... not recognized as a fully fledged adult. If she is unmarried or divorced she will be expected to take responsibility for the day to day running of the *mwenga* in which she lives, freeing her older female relatives to spend more time in the practice of any special skills they may possess (ibid.:38).

Women may dislike the supervision of the husband's kin, and this forms one of the reasons for marriage breakdown.

Between thirty-one and fifty-nine years of age, women can supervise work by younger women; the latter free the former to engage in "... specialized skilled activity using those traditional skills inherited from older relatives" (ibid.:40), while still being under the supervision of older women in some areas. To be regarded as true specialists, women (as men) must know the 'law' underlying the skill, presumably learned from older women. As for men in this age group, relations with older members of the same gender are more relations of cooperation than of supervision. Among the foods produced by women are two used in rituals. Women in this age group have limited "spare time," and make things while socializing in groups.

Beyond sixty years of age, women's productive position is similar to that of men's (see previous section). However, women seem to be more alert in their aged years than do men, whose pattern of activity has changed more radically as, perhaps, loss of mobility does not allow them to practice the skills they have learned (ibid.: 43), as we indicated before, and because colonialism has deprived them of much of the ritual activity in which they previously engaged.

Given the different post-marital residence pattern (according to informants), the picture for Banaban women would have been different, as it would have been for men. Geddes' description of work activity and inheritance (women tend to inherit poorer land than men; upon desertion, men have a greater claim to household articles than women) suggests that in certain respects North Tabiteuea—at least today—is more of a male-dominated society. However, it could still have been the case that the difference in the pattern of supervision, as between men, and between women, held on Banaba.

Similarly as for men: The appearance of a specifically female productive capacity should be understood in the context of relations between the genders and within genders. But there is a difference. Women are more closely supervised by other women.

For women, one can point to a similarity to men in the shift from supervision of the exercise of productive capacity, to use-rights in the products of that capacity and the time of its use. One can also point to younger women's work giving older women the time to further develop and engage their more fully specialized skills. An ethnographic mystery is where women's ritual activities should be located in this picture, since the emphasis in ritual activity associated with the 'meeting house' was on men.

However, the data from North Tabiteuea do suggest the notion of a greater continuity in women's subsistence activities through the life cycle than in men's, and a greater continuity between women's activities associated with subsistence and with procreative aspects of women's productive capacity.

Geddes presents time-budgets for a sample of men and women, but the time-budgets are difficult to use for the purposes of reconstruction given economic changes from precolonial times. Whether, in precolonial times, women's subsistence activities freed men to engage in ritual and bellicose activities is an obvious question which we cannot answer with any precision, for reasons of both methodology and of data.

*Cross-Gender.* But it is not only women who supervise other women. In at least some activities where adult men and women acted jointly, men supervised the activity of women and of other men. The matter becomes complex especially when we consider questions of sexual access to women, which I interpret as questions involving use-rights in women's procreative capacity.

We observed above that a particular burden of shame befell a young woman's mother if the young woman was found—by her new husband's female relatives—not to be a virgin at the time of her first marriage. The day-to-day responsibility to supervise a young woman's virginity thus appears to have been with her elder female kin.

Given material to be presented shortly, it is reasonable to interpret women's responsibility here as in a sense being "delegated" by men. This is in part because men supervised the bestowal of use-rights in the procreative capacities of both men and women. Various accounts conflict on whether arrangements for marriages were made by senior relatives, or by men. Often enough, "relatives" should be read as "men." But it is hard to see marriage arrangements as only involving men—certainly among Banabans today.

A kind of "middle position" is that while both men and women were involved in the bestowal of sexual use-rights, men had a supervisory position and were more generous about premarital liaisons when it came to other men than when it came to women.

For the general pattern, Grimble observed that men should not "communicate" (sexually?) with women until ritual made the men fit for marriage. Yet the virginity test he talks about is one for women. The people could, presumably, have invented some sort of virginity test for men if they had wanted to. Among Banabans at least today, there is a kind of sexual double standard. The virginity of the bride is at issue at marriage, not the virginity of the groom. The most complex set of descent unit activities still extant centers on marriage. If the bride is known not to be a virgin, people consider it beside the point to engage in these activities. One can suggest that as more effort went into keeping a woman a virgin than in keeping a man a virgin, the virgin woman was more valuable than the virgin man. This logic may also have been involved in the fact that in pre-colonial Banaban society, after a boy and girl were engaged, if the boy broke the engagement, his family gave lands to the girl's family, more if sexual relations had actually occurred. The girl's family did not give land to the boy's family if it was the girl who terminated the engagement.

In the course of events leading up to marriage during my period of field-work, the rule was: the groom's family proposes, the bride's family disposes (see a full discussion in Silverman 1971). The groom's family journeyed to the bride's family to discuss a proposal for marriage, which the bride's family accepted or rejected. There was a series of movements back and forth between the two families. As part of these, the wedding night was spent on the groom's side; there was some belief that the groom's side should name the first child.

The bilaterality of the system was indicated in the back and forth movements (the children would belong to both sides, and the bride and groom were told to regard their parents-in-law with solidarity, although the groom's family may have had some fear that the bride's family would 'pull' the groom away from them), as was the different position of men and women.

Geddes reports that on North Tabiteuea the husband must give the wife permission to travel beyond the household, and while away from the household she should be accompanied by kin. A woman without a husband usually travels with children or female kin, lest she invite gossip. One of the activities which takes women away from the household is taro cultivation; here, "... a woman is always accompanied by her husband, children or female kin. It is while being accompanied by younger women in the kin group that she is likely to pass on her knowledge to them so that they in turn become skilled in *babai* [taro] cultivation" (Geddes 1975: 40).

As far as we know, taro was not grown on Banaba, but women would have gone beyond their house sites to acquire fruit, enter water-caves (but only with other women), etc. In a documentary source there are statements, probably taken from an old Banaban in the 1920s or 1930s, which suggest that the wife was under the sexual hegemony of her husband and his male kin, and that part of the husband's sister's 'work' was to watch over the sexual conduct of her brother's wife so that the latter did not have sexual relations with the husband's unmarried brothers. Such relations were more or less tolerated by the husband according to his disposition, but the wife in question was said to be obliged to submit; this was probably an extreme statement (Silverman 1971: 301). [33]

It is reasonable to assume that the husband was the primary supervisor of his wife's sexual conduct, but that part of his responsibility was "delegated" to his female kin (as in the interpretation above, about the father and female kin), particularly (for Banaba) to his sister. Operating on this assumption, one aspect of the differentiation of a woman's procreative capacity from her other capacities could have been the practice of male supervision.

That what was going on was not exactly the same for men and for women is also suggested by the consequences of adultery: the husband claimed land from the offending man. This was the 'land of peace-making' referred to earlier. The land was a kind of substitute for the offender's life, which would have been taken had he been discovered before his house was broken up and his land taken (Maude and Maude 1932:289).

While childbirth involved women caring for women, according to Grimble the general pattern for the Gilberts included a special

activity for men. Upon birth, the father cut the umbilical cord
after the placenta emerged. If cut before, it was believed that the
loose end would "recede into the mother." The father cut the
cord with a battle lance and recited an incantation if the newborn
infant was a boy; the father just cut the cord with a stone chop-
ping block if the infant was a girl. The father literally separated
the child from its mother, as men later separated boys from
women.

During the three days following birth, mother and child remained in the north end of the house, where the birth had occurred. During this interval, the child (presumably whether male
or female) was being protected by a female spirit who lived in the
north. The mother's and father's families performed a ritual to
join the child's soul to its body, which joining seems to have occurred on the fourth day, in another house (ibid.:39). [34]

It was thus a female spirit who was protecting (might one say,
was supervising?) the child.

At death, the *bo-maki* ceremony was held for three nights,
perhaps paralleling the three day ceremony before the child's
soul was joined to its body. The ceremony at death was "... to
encourage the soul of the dead to leave the neighbourhood of the
body and also to drive away any evil spirit that might wish to
possess it" (ibid.:44). Women did special things here, as was
apparently also the case on Banaba.

> The privilege of attending to the corpse was generally claimed by the
> women of the household, though a loving son or grandson might also
> take part; no *tabu* lay upon the attendants when the task was done.
> Their first duty was to anoint the body from head to foot with coconut
> oil, which had been scented with flowers of the *uri* tree (*Guettarda speci-
> osa*), or with a handful of desiccated pith of the *kunikun* (wild almond).
> The latter substance was much used on Banaba, where almond trees grow
> profusely; it was greatly valued, as the wild almond was considered to
> be the favourite tree of the ancestral goddess Tituaa-bine, who dwelt in
> Matang, one of the bournes of departed souls (ibid.:45).

That ancestral goddess is also the one who, in dreams, brings
messages of death.

> On the third night, after the final performance of the *bo-maki* ceremony,
> one of the female relations of the deceased came to utter the final spells,

which would—to translate the Gilbertese idiom—'straighten the path of the soul to the land of ghosts'. She was called *te tia-tabe-atu* 'the lifter of the head', because she held the dead person's head in her lap while muttering the spell. If her work was well done, it was believed that the body appeared to shine like fire (possibly with the phosphorescence of decay) in the eyes of the soul, who turned away in fear and at once set out on his journey to the last bourne. If the body was kept for nine days, the *tia-tabe-atu* performed her office every evening, from the third to that preceding the day of burial (ibid.:46).

Before burial, the corpse was given a new waist mat and sleeping mat, and was garlanded. These objects were made by women.

Women thus not only supervised people's entry into the world, but also supervised their departure.

FROM THE POINT OF VIEW OF PRODUCTION:
REALIZING USE-VALUE

While there was a stress on the elder members of one gender supervising the work of the younger members of the same gender, and transmitting skills to them, we also find that each gender used products made by the other. This applies both to "means of production" and to "articles of consumption"(Marx 1967 [1867], vol. 2:395). For example, Banabans say that a sister was mat-maker for her brother, a brother was fisherman for his sister; a wife was mat-maker for her husband, a husband was fisherman for his wife.

Only men could fish beyond the Banaban reef. But a very highly prized form of fish-hook was made of materials at least some of which could only be acquired or made by women. In the Gilberts, women made certain things out of coconut toddy, which was acquired by men.

One would have to make a systematic inventory of things made and time spent in order to establish the point, but it seems reasonable to conclude that as each gender produced separately, it incorporated products made by the other; as each gender produced separately, in order to realize their use-value its products were shared with the other gender (as was also the case with procreation) in everyday life. [35]

The discussion of supervision in the last section suggests that the organization of work activities and the time devoted to them were functions not only of the "technical requirements" of the work involved, but also of the reproduction of gender relations of production, which included the relations of elders to juniors of the same gender.[36] This kind of statement presupposes that we can speak of gender in terms of genuine relations of production and not only as a feature of the organization of cooperation. This presupposition is warranted by the analysis of the "gender division of labor" as also a "gender division of property;" male tasks and female tasks were not only "fulfilled by" or "allocated to" men and women. Men had the capacity and the *right* to do certain things; women had the capacity and the *right* to do certain things; each needed the other to produce.

The relation between time and reproduction emerges clearly in the analysis of North Tabiteuea:

> Although Tabiteueans do not consciously use time it nevertheless appears that the amount of time spent in various kinds of activities is important in determining the recognized importance of the activity in relation to others. By this is meant that although the overall allocation of time to activities is not conscious, those activities considered important have built into them additional time use over that required to perform the essential tasks involved in achieving the desired results (Geddes 1975: 55).

As for the relation between time, reproduction and gender:

> The main difference between activities labeled "rest" and *"kakakibotu"* on Tabiteuea centred on the breadth of the kin group involved. Where *mwenga* members claimed to have 'rested' they often meant that they had spent time lying or sitting down inside their house in the company of other *mwenga* members idly chatting or simply sleeping. Where they referred to their activity as *'kakakibotu'* they included members of other *mwenga,* either *utu* ['kin'—MGS] or 'as if' kin, in the same sort of activity as was implied in the term 'rest' or *motirawa* (ibid.:57).

The "recreational" *(kakakibotu)* time is regarded as "well spent." Older people in particular regarded it as important, and: "The more senior a person is in a *mwenga* the more time will be set aside for this activity" (ibid.). People form recreational groups; members are usually linked through kinship or locality; they exchange information, enjoy one another's company and increase their solidarity.

These recreational groups are, however, usually composed of people of one gender who are over thirty years of age, and thus people who are supervising the work of others; the participation of younger people is discouraged. And: "The groups comprised of men usually represent a wider residential area comprised of more *mwenga* than the groups comprised of women" (ibid.:58).

We can put many of these observations together by suggesting that people operated with a set of notions of what we may call "socially necessary gender labor." And what was considered socially necessary labor was in part (to repeat) a function of the requirements of the reproduction of the relations of production, as manifested in *(inter alia)* the amount of time devoted to particular activities, especially if we include the time devoted to acquiring and developing the skills considered requisite for the optimal performance of those activities. [37]

As we have seen, these skills were usually acquired from, and their exercise was for quite a while supervised by, elders who had the time to do many of the things they did as younger people took over the performance of many day-to-day production activities which they had themselves done in their youth (some of these activities are at times termed "chores" in the literature). Becoming a good fisherman involved the acquisition of more skill and (I assume) the use of more time than, say, becoming a good coconut collector, and was regarded as a superior activity.

And here we come upon an important hint, which places questions about deep-sea fishing in the same critical context as questions about hunting raised in the analysis of peoples in other parts of the world. Catala wrote as follows in 1957:

It is often believed, partly because of the extensive activity formerly associated with deep sea fishing such as fishing for *Ruvettus* that the natives chiefly fish in the open ocean. Of course some fishes can usually be caught only at considerable depths—100 fathoms and over—and for others canoes must go several miles off-shore, as in bonito fishing. Around some northern islands the capture of flying fish and tuna involves rather elaborate means and great qualities of seamanship. But these spectacular operations are not everywhere a daily occupation. After observing the various fishing activities of these territories as best we could, we are now convinced that apart from these particular regional cases the fish supply of most Gilbertese populations is found much more frequently in the immediate vicinity of the land and in the shallows than far offshore. This observation is even more true of atoll islands, since the lagoon and especially its shallow parts are the most commonly frequented fishing grounds. It is also the place where a maximum subsistence may be found with a minimum of effort (Catala 1957:118).

Deep-sea fishing was the right of men; at least for North Tabiteuea, there is evidence that men also fished the deep lagoon (Geddes 1975:60). Colonial government regulations on canoe travel, and production for sale, were probably two of the factors which decreased the frequency of deep-sea fishing. Catala observes that fishing outside the reef in canoes "must have been the most popular" kind of fishing in the past (ibid.:125).

My understanding is that men in the Gilbert Islands proper, as among Banabans, represented deep-sea fishing as one of the premier, if not the premier, male subsistence activity. But one wonders about this. Fishing closer to shore, obtaining molluscs, etc., may have provided both a more regular part of the diet and a quantitatively important part of the diet (people say that on Banaba there was always good fishing beyond the reef, however). Catala observes that gathering shellfish was "the privilege of women and children" (Catala 1957:123), and that "a group of men, sometimes accompanied by a few women" engaged in net fishing in the lagoon (ibid.:128). Lambert notes that teams of "two or three men, and some married couples" search for small fish, octopi and eels at night in the Northern Gilberts. Young men and women also stocked fish ponds there (Lambert 1963: 19, 187). For North Tabiteuea in the Southern Gilberts, Geddes observes that members of the household hunt for fish on the lagoon flats. In daytime women and children look for fish. At night it becomes a household affair:

Though this is an important source of fish at certain times in each month most *mwenga* consider it a form of 'family sport' and the children become quite excited as the time approaches. This is probably one of the few *mwenga* activities in which all the active members of the *mwenga* are likely to participate (Geddes 1975:59).

Young men and women engage in net fishing in the lagoon;
older women participate but not older men (ibid.). As for canoe
fishing:

> Most men regard canoe fishing as a sport which happens to be useful,
> a woman may often say 'He has been out playing' when talking about
> her husband's fishing trip. However, sitting on a canoe through the middle
> of a tropical day with the sun reflecting off the water can be a very hot
> and uncomfortable experience (ibid.:62).

I think that the points raised above have interesting implications for "thinking" the labor theory of value in some precapitalist formations (cf. Godelier 1977:chapters 4, 5 and 9). It is as
if these people operated with a kind of "gender labor" theory of
the evaluation of work activities, in which, for example, men's
deep-sea fishing was an activity superior to women and children
collecting shellfish; older men's or women's activities in which
they exercised their highly developed skills were superior to the
activities of younger people who had not yet perfected such skills.

The elders who supervised the work of same-gender juniors
were not anybody, but were kin and affines (whom for these
purposes we can consider, generally speaking, people with use-
rights of various kinds in each other's productive capacities,
products and property). Given this point and the data on the
organization of work, we can see certain concrete relationships
(e.g., father and son, mother and daughter, husband and wife)
and gender relations themselves being immediately reproduced
in the work process and in the everyday sharing of products.

## FROM THE POINT OF VIEW OF REPRODUCTION

In his chapter on "simple reproduction" in *Capital,* volume one,
Marx wrote:

> Whatever the form of the process of production in a society, it must be
> a continuous process, must continue to go periodically through the same
> phases. A society can no more cease to produce than it can cease to con-
> sume. When viewed, therefore, as a connected whole, and as flowing on
> with incessant renewal, every social process of production is, at the same
> time, a process of reproduction.
>
> The conditions of production are also those of reproduction. No

society can go on producing, in other words, no society can reproduce, unless it constantly reconverts a part of its products into means of production, or elements of fresh products. All other circumstances remaining the same, the only mode by which it can reproduce its wealth, and maintain it at one level, is by replacing the means of production—i.e., the instruments of labour, the raw material, and the auxiliary substances consumed in the course of the year—by an equal quantity of the same kind of articles; these must be separated from the mass of the yearly products, and thrown afresh into the process of production. Hence, a definite portion of each year's product belongs to the domain of production. Destined for productive consumption from the very first, the portion exists, for the most part, in the shape of articles totally unfitted for individual consumption (Marx 1967 [1867] :566).

As we will see, through the incest taboo, both men and women were "thrown afresh" into the process of production. But they were not "thrown afresh" in exactly the same way, as by now we have good reason to expect.

I would like to develop the following line of interpretation: Given marriage and the incest taboo, correct procreation is the production of children who could further procreate children and thus preserve or replenish what was transmitted to them or expended for them, and who could reproduce. On the same logic, the spouses of a sibling set, through new production, reproduce, and preserve what was transmitted from the parents of the sibling set. [38] In order to establish this point we will have to establish a few others.

*The Terms For Procreation and Incest.* In Gilbertese, *kariki* as a verb means 'to engender, to create, to procreate, to conceive, to invent, to institute'. As a noun, it means 'progeny, procreation, posterity, descent, issue, race'. The term can be analyzed as being composed of 'to cause', plus 'to be born, to come into existence, to originate, to develop, to take form, to germinate; more, again, in addition'.

It is very tempting to regard procreation as the exemplary form of new production by people, and to regard one's child as the exemplary new product among products. This product is a person rather than a thing. And in producing it, one's relation to it is not severed; one also 'develops it, makes it grow'.

The suffix *-ra* means 'bad, inappropriate, impure, disagreeable'.

Incest is *karikira (kariki + -ra)*, or in a euphonic form, *kanikira*. *Karikira* means 'incest' or 'to commit incest', and also 'born of incest, misshapen, deformed, incestuous progeny' (Sabatier 1954: 390). The meanings of the term have to do with bad procreation, in the sense of the act of doing it and the outcome. [39]

I do not think it takes many interpretive leaps to see a relation being expressed between incest and procreation and between procreation and production, especially the production of something new and additional to what already exists.

In order to understand aspects of why some people rather than others 'procreate badly', we will have to look at a few kin terms.

*Kin Terms.* If we look at the terms for consanguines from a generational point of view, we find the following: in ego's own generation, ego distinguishes people according to whether they are of the same gender as ego ('same gender siblings' and 'different gender siblings'). [40] In the first ascending generation, ego distinguishes between men and women ('mothers' and 'fathers'). In the first descending generation, we have 'children'. At two generations removal, we have 'grandperson' (grandparent or grandchild). [41] There is a further set of reciprocals between people of more distant generations. Those terms are formed by adding suffixes to the grandperson term, and the grandperson term can be used for them too. 'Grandperson' thus applies to any person two or more generations distant; grandparent and grandchild are the exemplary grandpersons. [42]

We can think of these terms as describing members of two-party relationships. In this way, the relationships are: (1) 'same gender sibling' and 'same gender sibling', 'different gender sibling' and 'different gender sibling'; (2) 'father' and 'child', 'mother' and 'child'; (3) 'grandperson' and 'grandperson'.

In relationships in one's own generation, the gender of both parties is terminologically relevant. For relationships between adjacent generations, the gender of one party (the senior) is terminologically relevant, the gender of the other party is neutralized. For relationships between alternate generations and beyond, the gender of both parties is neutralized. [43]

Terms are as eloquent in their absence as in their presence. There is no pair of terms (taking a pair as describing a relationship) in which one party is specifically male and the other party is

specifically female (such as 'brother' and 'sister' in English).
There is no pair describing a consanguineal relationship in which
both parties are specifically either male or female (such as the
English 'brother' and 'brother', or 'sister' and 'sister').

Such pairs only occur where affines are involved. These are:
(1) 'brother-in-law' and 'brother-in-law' between men; the term
also means in-law in general; brothers-in-law are the exemplary
in-laws; (2) 'sister-in-law' and 'sister-in-law' between women.
Reciprocal specific gender occurs in the context of marriage. [44]

*The Banaban Incest Taboo.* The Maudes wrote: "A Banaban
was prohibited from marrying his direct ascendants, or the issue
of his direct ascendants, up to and including his (or her) great-
grandparents" (Maude and Maude 1932:269). H.E. Maude also
states this as the general boundary for the Gilberts (Maude 1963:
61). [45]

A Gilbertese phrase which sums up the situation is usually translated as 'the fourth generation goes free', possibly following
Grimble's translation. The 'fourth generation' part can also be
glossed as 'the fourth generation to come into being'. [46] The 'goes
free' part can also be glossed as 'leaps out, spreads out, procreates,
leaves one place for another'. [47] Thus: the fourth generation to
come into being goes free, leaps out, spreads out, procreates,
leaves one place for another.

*The Incest Taboo Explored.* To carry the analysis forward
requires the making of some assumptions. These are not *a priori*
assumptions, but assumptions which are at least somewhat
grounded in the ethnography as interpreted so far.

The first assumption (a very conventional one) is that we can
link up a variety of apparently different practices into a pattern;
particularly, that we can link up the interpretation of the incest
taboo with the interpretation of other things about production.

The second assumption is that we take seriously the idea that
the grandchild generation has a special link of sameness with the
grandparent generation. Making this assumption means that the
terminological equivalence of relationships generationally more
distant than grandparent-grandchild is not being given the same
interpretive significance as the terminological equivalence of
grandparent-grandchild. I am taking this step as a development of
Grimble's points on the identification of alternate generations, the

ethnography of the grandparent-grandchild relation as Grimble
presented it, and the fact that the 'grandperson' term indeed can
be used for relationships of more than two generations' distance.

The third assumption is that we take seriously the direct reference of the incest term to procreation, and, even more specifically,
to the production of new people. Phrased otherwise, the concept
of incest links sexual relations with the production of new people,
and the production of new people is the exemplary aspect of
production.

The fourth assumption is that we take seriously the way 'the
fourth generation' is constructed, as 'the fourth generation which
comes into being'. On this assumption, the image is not of generations in a layer cake arrangement, but in directional, generational
time. Interestingly enough, the suffix which makes 'grandperson'
into 'greatgrandperson' in other uses means 'erection', usually
of the penis, which suggests both procreation and maleness. The
suffixes for the even more distant generations suggest the increasing decrepitude of the senior party. [48]

Thus the fifth assumption, which is that we take seriously the
'leaps out, spreads out, procreates, leaves one place for another'
part of the statement of the prohibition.

Given these assumptions and the previous analysis, then: procreation was reproduction in the double sense of the production
of a new child and thus new procreative capacity, and the preservation of what was transmitted from the parent's parent to the
parent. The identification of alternate generations was the preservation aspect. The observance of the incest taboo was the new
production aspect. [49] In order for the grandchild to constitute
new production, it had to be the product of new production:
that of the child's spouse. In order for that spouse's production
to be new, the spouse could not be related to the child as a descendant of the parent's grandparents. That would be nothing new (cf.
Hooper 1976, Labby 1976b), and the spouses would be preserving
what had already been preserved, whether one thinks of what had
already been preserved as capacities, persons, use-values, substances, generations or relationships.

Looked at from the perspective of the sibling set, we can say
that the spouses of a sibling set through new production preserve
what was transmitted from the parents of the sibling set. [50]

Labby's interpretation of incest among the Yapese (Labby 1976b) demonstrates that the Yapese associate incest with cannibalism, and that both represent a kind of self-consumption (cf. Hooper 1976, on Tahiti). There is no direct evidence for such an association among the Banabans. But there is such evidence for the Gilbertese, among whom the incest taboo in ancient times applied to a wider range of kin (and in some communities today applies to a wider range), and the notion of incest itself applied to a wider range of phenomena. Grimble wrote of exogamous patrilineal sibs in the Gilberts (but on the question of patrilineality, see Lundsgaarde and Silverman 1972), descended from or closely connected to one or more totems. "The eating of the totem, or its desecration, was once considered a form of incest" (Grimble 1933-1934:14). He also wrote:"No member of a sib may eat the totem-creature of his group; the creature is held to be flesh of his flesh, and its use as food is considered to be the first step toward incest" (ibid.:20). Among the Banabans, whether or not harming or eating the embodiments of ancestral spirits was considered incest, it was prohibited.

There is thus at least support from Grimble's writings on the Gilbertese for the kind of interpretation Labby makes.

What we do not know is whether these people believed that in some sense an aspect of substance was consumed as the parent transmitted substance to the child. If they did, then the new substance which the spouse adds which is transmitted to the child may have truly been considered to replenish something, as well as to preserve something, which was transmitted from the grandparents. [51]

*"Material."* Let us presume the line of interpretation developed in the last section, and link it with a hint from the proverbial position of the Banaban son-in-law by assuming that children (seen not only individually but also as members of sibling sets) produce to meet their own consumption needs and those of their dependents (especially their children); the consumption needs of those who are producing or have produced for them in everyday life (especially parents and grandparents), thus replenishing the latter; and furthermore produce a surplus to be "socialized" in reproduction. Let us take this assumption and link it to the discussion of gender "material" production by assuming that the manner in

which children could do this itself presupposes the gender pattern: in particular, children were obliged to the father and mother, and the way in which they 'untie their debts' must have been different for sons and daughters. Let us further assume that, to a degree, children could go about doing this by utilizing the work and products of kin on whose productive capacity they had a claim.

Given the orientation of the system to both symmetry and asymmetry from the gender point of view, and given the importance of having not one child or children of one sex but a sibling set of both sons and daughters (Silverman 1971), the following picture emerges: Daughters fulfilled their obligations to their parents through their own work (and products) and that of their husbands, children and brothers; sons fulfilled their obligations to their parents through their own work (and products) and that of their wives, children and sisters. The specific ways in which particular men and women were organized in this regard was a consequence of their specific situations.

From the Gilbertese side, where there is more a stress on virilocal residence and the continuity between father and son, we can obtain an image of the general way in which the system worked. Grimble observed (see above) that a father might send his son to look after an elder (male) relative as a companion, since the father was a "busy breadwinner" and could not afford to do it himself. As sons could have guardian grandfathers, daughters could have guardian grandmothers, although it is more difficult to gain a picture of them from Grimble. But Geddes' data on gender activities and their supervision allow one to suggest that people could produce for their parents in part through their children, who worked under close supervision, and that this work was one of the things which enabled the elders to engage their "specialized skills." The use of these skills by the elder generation on behalf of the junior itself constituted a kind of new production which set up a further obligation on the part of the junior generation. The exercise of very special care toward elder generation set up a further obligation on the part of the elder generation, which the latter discharged through the giving of special lands and skills to the junior.

One of the preconditions for these possibilities is a limited substitutability of the work and products of members of the same gender. [52] This substitutability is well-documented. For example, in the Southern Gilberts today where a family has difficulty supporting the number of children that it has, the family can have some of their children fostered by relatives who will look after them; the children do "household chores" for the foster parents. Lundsgaarde cites the case of a man whose wife was incapacitated and they only had a son; the man's nephew's daughter came to help in the house, while the man gave her food and clothing (Lundsgaarde 1966:91).

In the Northern Gilberts today:

> When the youngest children have grown up, the parents usually retire from active life and are supported in turn by each of their sons and daughters. An aged husband and wife may even live in separate households. If there is only one child, or only one son, living on the island, the younger couple may gradually take over the management of the parental household instead of establishing its own home elsewhere (Lambert 1963:106).

In the Northern Gilberts siblings have closer property relations with one another than was the case on Banaba, holding a joint estate for some time. In the South there were also such joint estates. Also in the North and elsewhere: "Siblings still rely on one another for unstinting assistance in material goods and labor. A sibling's adolescent son or daughter is often 'borrowed' to help with the work in an overburdened household" (Lambert 1970: 265). When a woman is pregnant or nursing, her husband's unmarried sister might come to do some of the wife's work (her own sister is riskier as the husband might try to seduce her; Lambert 1963:104). A man who cannot find a wife, whom he needs to work, may live with his parents, especially his mother. A mother may continue doing "chores" for a son without a wife (Lambert 1966:114).

This substitutability of gender "material" labor, occurring within and limited by the kinds of social relations people had (i.e., relations in which people had use-rights in one another's material productive capacity, products, property) may be seen vis-à-vis an even more limited substitutability from the point of view of use-rights in procreative capacity. The substitutability is more limited in that from the material point of view both consanguines and affines of the same gender can do many of the same things, whereas from the procreative point of view only some affines could—i.e., there was the possibility of sexual relation between people and some relatives-in-law of opposite gender.[53] The "material" and "procreative" sides were themselves linked in the context of childbirth, when a man might have had sexual relations with a wife's sister, while his wife, when pregnant or nursing, was being looked after by female relatives.

As far as socialized surplus for reproduction is concerned we should look to claims which people had to one another's productive capacity associated with requests or gifts between kin, and with certain aspects of the "descent system." In order to explicate these we will first have to discuss the transmission of land more specifically. But we can note at this point that many foreign observers of the Gilbertese (and of some other Pacific Islanders) have observed how kinsfolk can ask one another (bubuti) for certain foods, clothing, household articles, and how it is difficult to refuse such requests—refusal being tantamount to a denial of the relationship. At the same time, I believe there is a general assumption that such requests should be "reasonable," that they should not compromise the donor's ability to meet his or her own needs and more immediate obligations (cf. Lambert 1963:44). Even if "the accounts" between kin "balance out" in the long run, it still may be possible to regard the practice as involving the production of a relative surplus which is socialized— especially as the practice has been interpreted as operating to prevent individuals from accumulating too much (see, e.g., Lundsgaarde 1966:68).

*The Transmission of Property: Land.* We will now continue the discussion of production and reproduction by showing how land could be transmitted so that existing property relations were preserved while further property could be transmitted:

Inheritance and use practices are variable from island to island in the Gilbertese-speaking area (see Lambert 1971). The more individualized-lineal Banaban practice of inheritance contrasts most sharply with the Northern Gilberts where a system prevailed which shared a number of features with feudal systems. I will focus in on a sketch of relevant aspects of the Banaban system, introducing a few bits of information from elsewhere along the way.

From this point of view of reproduction, the transmission of rights to land presents interesting and complex problems:

It was noted earlier that there was a concrete relation between use-right and inheritance, in that generally speaking children had use-rights in the lands of their parents, and on Banaba the parents subdivided most of their lands among their children when the children matured. From the children's perspective, use-right became ownership, to some of the parents' lands. From the proprietor's perspective, ownership included the right to allow others to use land. On some islands people were given use-rights to trees planted on the lands of others. A person had use-rights in the spouse's lands which could extend after the spouse's death when there were children to support.

Even where land was more individually owned, close kin had residual inheritance rights in one another's lands. As an example, imagine the following situation for Banaba. Ego has lands transmitted from his mother, Nei T, and from his father, Nam B. T and B have died but they have siblings. Ego has no children, and did not transfer lands in his lifetime to others At his death, his lands from Nei T will be divided among her siblings (or perhaps their children), while the lands from Nam B will be divided among his siblings (or their children). Kin such as these also have some measure of control over how people can transmit their lands outside the usual channel of transmitting them to children. These rights of close kin may relate to what has been described for the Gilberts (where such residual rights and limitations to transfer also obtain) as partial use-rights which kin have in one another's lands.

The point I am moving toward is illuminated by Banaban adoption practices. The least ambiguous form of adoption, as an adoption, is the adoption of another person as child, especially where the child receives no land from the natal parents. The most ambiguous form of adoption, as an adoption (and it may be a recent form) is where a person adopts another person (perhaps a step-parent) as parent, effectively giving that person use-rights in some land. But whether the adopted parent had the right to transmit that land to other people was unclear (e.g., should the adopted parent have children with a spouse who is not the adopter's parent; see Silverman 1970). For the Southern Gilberts, Lundsgaarde observes:

> If an adopted child dies without issue, the land received in adoption will revert back to the nearest consanguineal relatives of the adopter. This implies that title to a parcel of land conveyed to an adopted child can only vest when the adoptee has offspring of his own (Lundsgaarde 1974:196; for a discussion of contrasting practices see Lambert 1971:164 et seq.)

For at least some of the islands, including Banaba, the point can be generalized by proposing that the transmission of land was a practice involving (a) *three* lineal parties—past holder, present holder and future holder, and (b) close kin who are residual heirs, who have some say in how the land can be transmitted, and who have some use-rights in the land itself. From the perspective of a particular landowner—in general and not only in adoption—the statement of ownership is most complete when the land has been transmitted to somebody else, usually to a child. We noted above that on North Tabiteuea a woman, at least, was regarded as a full adult when she had a child. "Moving" things to the next generation thus secured the position of one's own.

If the "three party" interpretation of inheritance is correct, then we encounter another dimension of the tri-generational relation which emerged in the discussion of the incest taboo.

Can we now extend the argument on production and reproduction to see how additional rights to property could be transmitted? I think we can:

In the normal course of events among Banabans my child inherits land from myself and from my wife. From my point of view and that of my family, my child will have use-rights in land that is not ours, and will inherit land that is not ours—as from my wife's point of view and that of her family, her child (who is of course also my child) will have use-rights in land that is not theirs, and will inherit land that is not theirs. Both families can win— and this may be related to the fractionation of landholdings.

Now, if we posit a link between the incest taboo, marriage and property (cf. Labby 1976a, 1976b), what the system implies is that from the point of view of co-descendants ("the level of the firm," as it were), people should transmit land to their children and, when they bear children, enlarge the land rights for those children from outside the range of the incest taboo. If people married inside the range their children would inherit land already possessed by co-descendants inside it, and becoming further fractionated among them and reduced in size of holdings per person if not in number of plots owned. This implies accumulational possibilities. What this amounts to from a slightly different structural angle is that from the perspective of each of the two families involved in a marriage, the process is one in which the endowment of procreative use-rights for one generation is succeeded by the acquisition of new land rights for the next, at the same time as each generation completes the inheritance of the generation which preceded it. [54]

*The Transmission of Property: From Land to Water and the "Descent System."* The subsistence lands which people owned were part of larger locales which were the loci of bilateral descent units. The question of precisely how membership in the units was established, sustained and transmitted is a complex one. In general terms, we can say that membership was dealt with in the same terms as kin relationships were dealt with: membership involved the sharing of common substance, the sharing of a relation to the land which was the locus of the descent unit and a record of participation in unit activities. The descent units were referred to by the name of the ancestor ('the issue of B'), or by the name of the territory, or by either, or by both. The substance and land were transmitted through intermediate generations from the original ancestor. [55]

There were five original ancestors, and the people maintained bilateral genealogies extending down from the ancestors to the time of the living. Each ancestor was the founder of a district. The districts were composed of hamlets, and at times there were sub-districts or coalitions of hamlets within a district. At specific points the descent lines within the genealogies and the territorial divisions coincided. For example, B was the original ancestor who founded district W. Three generations since B there was a sibling set of four and each of the four siblings was the founder of a hamlet.

The district had one or more meeting houses and spirit houses, terraces and *kouti* sites. Each hamlet (or at least many hamlets) had a 'seat' in the meeting house and spirit house, a special place where its members would sit.

From the point of view of production narrowly construed, it is suitable to see the units as units within which people had access to life-sustaining resources.

The water caves were tied to the hamlets. I do not know whether every hamlet had a cave. The descendants of the cave's discoverer looked after the cave, but the members of the discoverer's hamlet were entitled to get water from it after asking the members of the discoverer's family (Maude and Maude 1932:291-292). Banaba was subject to periodic, often devastating droughts, and these caves were considered to be even more valuable than land (ibid.). Only women could actually enter the caves and draw water (for everyday consumption and in drought); this they did in groups, and such groups were one of the most regular collective subsistence task groups. [56] It is worthy of note that the ritual at the time of birth, marriage and death seems to have occurred at the hamlet level, and those activities were activities in which women had a special place.

Fishing seems to have been tied to the district in some ways. The men's canoe sheds were on the district's terrace, and presumably, when the weather was favorable, canoes could be launched from the foreshore of the district. [57] A variety of ritual activities which occurred at the district level were activities in which men had a special place.

While speaking of "levels" of units is a simplification, we can see a hint of a connection between gender productive capacities and what units of apparently different orders did: between what women did and the hamlet; between what men did and the district. It is tempting to draw a picture of an increasing communalization of access as one moves from land resources (engaging men and women, through the descent line), downward to the underground water caves (engaging women, through the hamlet), and outward to the sea (engaging men, through the district). Communalization of access is greater where the genders are most distinct in their activities.

The "descent system" appears as a concrete *system* because different units had particular prerogatives in activities which linked the units with one another. It appears as a logical system because one can discern similar principles "operating" in the organization of different units—principles which are in turn similar to principles operating in other contexts (e.g., siblingship, parent and child relations) which involve the sharing of common substance and the possession of inter-linked land rights. The principles include assumptions about the implications of gender, age and generation.

The Banabans distinguish between matters associated with "ordinary kinship" and the prerogatives of the descent system, while the people also recognize the relations between them. One way in which we can pose the relations between the two is as follows: As rights of residual heirship become more distant in their likelihood of being exercised, which has a close connection to collateral kinship distance, the use-rights of kin in one another's (surplus?) productive capacities attenuate (unless kin decide otherwise on special grounds). This increasing attentuation roughly corresponds to an increasing *contextualization* of their relationship, so that these days their intense interactions specifically grounded in that relationship focus around what I have termed "family gatherings"—e.g., gatherings at times of birth, first menstruation, marriage and death. At these occasions, relatives bring or send gifts to 'help with the work' of the gathering (see full discussion in Silverman 1971).

At least these days people keep accounts, so that if you (and perhaps your siblings) bring ten shillings to my family gathering, I will be expected to bring ten shillings to your family gathering (people say that in the old days the presentations were of food). While this appears as a calculated exchange, and in a sense is a calculated exchange, people say that they 'contribute' to 'help with the work', such as feeding the people who are there—of course including those who come to help with the work. Previously I reacted rather arrogantly to the local explanation, looking for deeper meanings behind a kind of sociological tautology (Silverman 1971). I think I was in error. It is something of a sociological tautology, as we are dealing with 'contributions' (or "exchange") within the area of relative surplus. It is not a tautology in the sense that in the old days, what probably enabled that surplus to occur, if one follows the links of the chain far enough, was the supervision and control of the work of younger people by older people of the same gender.

In the old days, as noted above, these gatherings seem to have occurred at the "hamlet level." Hamlets were also involved in the system of prerogatives. The operation of the system of prerogatives, drawing in even more distant kin, was usually limited to specific contexts in which there was not only a differentiation of activities, but also a hierarchical structure of supervision. While the activities and the structure of supervision were highly contextualized (at least in theory), the matters with which they dealt were, from the point of view of reproduction, very important. The contexts may also have been those in which, through their contributions, individuals and families could take rightful pride in their productivity and skill, such expressions elsewhere making people seem 'pushy' in the eyes of their fellows (cf. Lundsgaarde 1966:68).

Specific hamlets had specific prerogatives in the organization of activities in the meeting house and spirit house, and in the maintenance of the houses. For example, hamlet B initiated activities, hamlet C provided fish for feasts, hamlet D made belts for dances, hamlet E made the thatch for the meeting house when the old thatch rotted. One of the regular activities at the spirit house was the collection of food from the different hamlets, which food was offered to the ancestral gods.

Relations between districts, or between hamlets of different districts, appear to have involved two sorts of activities primarily: the incorporation of "external windfalls" into island social relations, and games. When certain things appeared off the island or on the foreshore (e.g., particular fish, turtle, strangers, flotsam and jetsam), not just anybody could take them as their own. A complex system of district and hamlet prerogatives was invoked. For example, a certain fish was found on the foreshore of district W. It had to be taken to sub-district X-1 of district X. Hamlet W-1 carried the head of the fish and hamlet W-2 carried the tail of the fish (W-1 and W-2 being hamlets of district W). Hamlet X-1 received the fish, and hamlet X-2 (another hamlet of district X) divided the fish up among the members of the participating hamlets.

There is little available detailed data on the games which were part of this system, but they were "... all the popular adult pastimes of the island" (Maude and Maude 1932:287). The senior

village district (for certain purposes) had the right to regulate
when the games would occur, according to the Maudes' account,
and there was a complex of rights similar to those regarding external windfalls. (For example, sub-district X-1 of the senior
district had to open the season for a particular game and could
then be challenged by hamlet Y-1 of district Y; another hamlet
had the prerogative of keeping score.)

Prerogatives belonged to units, and were described by words
meaning activity, work, manner, custom, right, property. Members' rights to enact those prerogatives were similarly described
(we can consider these rights as use-rights, but will not use that
term much as its usage becomes clumsy). The rights of all members of a unit in its prerogatives were not the same. The Maudes
referred to the senior member of the village district as the "chief,"
a usage contested by many contemporary Banabans, perhaps
because it suggests to them a generalized authority in matters of
everyday life, as opposed to having certain prerogatives in this
system. The Maudes indeed spoke of the chief's "definite but
limited powers," which included speaking first in the meeting
house, and having considerable influence in making arrangements
for district activities. [58]

There was a general rule of succession to the position of seniority by primogeniture. But if the eldest child was a daughter,

the nearest male descendant or relative will perform the functions of the
chiefship until the daughter has a son who can do the work. The daughter
will be called chiefess until her death, when her son will take over the title
as well as the duties of the office, the Banabans considering that these
duties are such that they cannot be performed by a female (Maude and
Maude 1932:73-74).

Let us now draw together some of the pieces which indicate how
descent unit activities operated in terms of reproduction.

The first thing to call attention to is that on all the reported
ritual occasions, people ate together. The Maudes described the
spirit house as a giant communal eating house. This food was
itself new production. The offering of food to the ancestors was
also an important aspect of the ritual activities, and there were
some "first fruits" rituals (cf. Maude 1963:37-38).

The second thing to call attention to is that many aspects of

the content of relations between descent units were regarded as
continuing the relations between the units' founders. For example,
assume that E and Y were siblings. E was the eldest sibling and Y
was a younger sibling. On general principles, the descendants of
E had the prerogative of initiative, and the descendants of Y
had a lesser prerogative, such as cleaning up the thatch in the
spirit house. Or, the parent gave a particular group of prerogatives
to E and another group of prerogatives to Y. In the normal course
of events, the descendants of E enacted E's prerogatives, and the
descendants of Y enacted Y's prerogatives. This was so especially
if there was an unbroken chain of enactments by those people
from the time of the founder to the time of the living.

Thus, a third thing to call attention to is that when people did
allow the enactment of their prerogatives to lapse, when they did
not involve themselves in new production, their membership
began to lapse—that is, the possibility decreased that others would
validate their claims to use and transmission. It is at this point that
the descent system and actual land ownership come together
again, as there are hints of people who 'left' a hamlet for greater
involvement in another one, with negative consequences both for
the transmission of land and the transmission of prerogatives.

*Separations and Conflict.* Various aspects of the enactment
of prerogatives indicate a precedence of males over females,
genealogically senior lines over genealogically junior lines, older
genealogical generations over junior genealogical generations,
older people over younger people, and people who have a long
record of enacting their rights over people who did not have such
a record. [59]

The precise relation between the transmission and enactment
of rights in this system was, however, variable and often problematic. The possibility of a variety of conflicts of interest was
generated. These conflicts of interest were often articulated
around the implications for succeeding generations of what people
were and did in anterior generations, and the implications of what
people are and do for the reproduction of what came before. Let
us explore this point briefly.

In the descent system, the general sibling relationship of the
founders of units was to be preserved by their descendants. But
differences in gender, birth order, age and generation were rele-

vant to how that preservation took place, to the question of precisely who could enact the prerogatives. Here a number of difficulties emerged.

The Maudes stated that if the senior member (we might say: transmitter) of a district were a woman, a male relative would enact her prerogatives until she had a son who could enact them. The actual situation was more complex. We find instances where, at least for some time, the descendants of a brother enacted his prerogatives and the descendants of a sister enacted her prerogatives; where the descendants of an elder sister, not of her junior brother, enacted the prerogative of initiative; where the prerogative of initiative of an elder sister was enacted by her male relatives and was returned to her line; where that prerogative of an elder sister was enacted by her male relatives but was not returned to her line (Silverman 1971).

Thus, there was not a consistent pattern when we raise the question of which men and which women in the succeeding generation 'actively related toward' things transmitted from men and women in the anterior generation.

On Banaba, at least as far as the senior lines of districts or hamlets were concerned, it is likely that there were many struggles in situations which appear to involve the conflict of different principles: for example, between primogeniture, men having the initiative and people transmitting what they had to their children.

The case was probably very similar for genealogical generation and age, which were conflated with seniority in a general notion of priority. Assume that E was of a senior genealogical generation, and Y was of a junior genealogical generation. It could have been the case that Y was very much younger than E, in which case E's relatives may have asserted that Y could not properly enact the prerogatives (a conflict between chronological age and genealogical generation), and possibly Y should not even transmit the prerogatives to Y's children. Or E could have been a woman and Y a man (a conflict between gender and seniority of generation). Or perhaps E's predecessors did not participate much in descent unit affairs, while Y's predecessors did participate (a conflict between exercise of rights and seniority of generation). It is likely that in pre-colonial times as in colonial times, people argued and at times fought their cases around such points (Silverman 1971).

Here we can develop a point which has occurred a number of times: production had to be new to preserve or reproduce what already existed. As one was producing anew, one was exercising one's productive capacity in relation to something; one was 'actively relating toward' something, enacting use-rights in something, or one was being permitted to enact those rights by someone who had them.

But 'actively relating toward' still had two sides: the actively relating, and the toward. They were unified in a single process, but, given the separations, that process was separated into different moments. People separated these moments, people also put them together. The separations and the issues around which conflict articulated also presupposed each other. Without the separations, there would not have been an issue around which conflict would articulate. Quite possibly, without issues around which conflict would articulate, there would not have been the same separations. [60]

*The Descent System and Socialized Surplus.* But there is more to be said about external windfalls and games. My choice of "external windfalls" to describe the object of many descent unit activities and prerogatives is a tendentious one (if not unprecedented; see below). As soon as we think of windfalls we can easily begin thinking of surplus. We can think of these windfalls as a kind of unproduced surplus which had to be socialized, but according to very detailed relations of supervision and rights to the items concerned. Phrasing the category in that way allows a solution to an otherwise (at least to me) intractable problem: how to construct theoretically the relation between the windfalls and the games.

Lambert provides a clue when he writes of Butaritari, a highly stratified Gilbertese island:

> Stranded porpoises were a windfall for a people whose craving for fat was seldom satisfied. Certain villages had ramages of porpoise-callers who possessed magic formulas for bringing these mammals onto the reef. I learned of the disposal of a large school in the 1920s from a contemporary account in a mission newspaper. The porpoises came ashore below the village of Kuuma; the inhabitants retained enough meat for their own feast, and sent the rest to the high chief Na Kaiea II in Butaritari Town, who distributed the meat among the households of the villages round about.

The particularly fatty back portion of a porpoise was reserved for the high chief himself (Lambert 1966:168).

Lambert's phrasing of the following point should be seen in terms of his disagreement with Sahlins, who related the presence of an aristocracy in Polynesia to the existence of a surplus, the "redistributive" function of chiefs with regard to primary food-stuffs, the growth of productivity, and the necessity for a group of people to administer the movement of goods.

> In summary, the gifts made to the high and petty chiefs originally had little economic significance, either for the donors or for the recipients. The presentations of food were only a very small proportion of a ramage's large taro plants, and even less of its other crops. Breadfruit, the staple for half the year, and such everyday foods as coconuts, pandanus, and the smaller varieties of taro were omitted, or included only incidentally. ... The redistribution of gifts of food on Butaritari and Makin can be interpreted as a demonstration of a relationship between a chief and his subjects. People brought huge taro corms to weddings, births, home-comings, sickbeds, and funerals in order to claim ramage membership or the future assistance of kinsmen (Lambert 1966:170).

Indeed, very large swamp taro tubers "... are perhaps more important as objects of display than as items of food. A wide range of social relationships sooner or later carry an obligation to contribute a predetermined amount of Cyrtosperma to a feast" (Lambert 1963:163). For North Tabiteuea, not as highly strati-fied as Butaritari and closer in many ways to the general situation on Banaba, Geddes observes that this form of taro is a "ceremonial food" and not important as an element of the daily diet (as the smaller type of this form of taro was on Butaritari), and much time is put into growing it (Geddes 1975; cf. Lundsgaarde 1966).

But perhaps the most remarkable fact of all about this taro is that the plant "... is in fact the only crop actually cultivated by the Gilbertese" (Catala 1957:67). Can one not say that people had to work with it for it to be able to serve its purposes?

There is no exact parallel with Banaba because of the lack of taro there. But Lambert's and Geddes' data suggest that the pro-duct singled out for "ceremonial occasions," many of them similar to the Banaban "family gatherings," is in the Northern Gilberts also the product which has a special importance in demonstrating the relation between chief and subject. This product, furthermore, was one that was *not* a part of the ordinary diet. It was cultivated (and other crops were not really cultivated in the same sense) largely to be used for such purposes, and growing it took a great deal of time and skill, which probably depended on younger people "freeing" older people to have that time and to develop that skill. And furthermore again, on Butaritari the high chief's rights included the rights to the stranded porpoise, which was one of the "windfall rights" on Banaba.

This taro on Butaritari may not be seen as a surplus appropriated by the high chief, but it can be seen as part of a *socialized surplus*. This interpretation is supported by the fact that the product was not produced for the immediate consumption of the producers or people close to them. Given the foregoing and Geddes' point on the relation between the importance of a product, the skills involved in utilizing it and time, we can look back to the interpretation of the relation between external windfalls and games on Banaba, the games which were "all the popular adult pastimes." They link in that the windfalls were an unproduced surplus from outside the community—an unproduced surplus which became "socialized" through the operation of the descent groups; and the games were a very particular kind of socialized surplus time, or even socialized surplus labor, from within the community itself, also socialized in the same manner. [61] The descent unit prerogatives can thus be seen as involving the development, supervision and control of socialized surplus, at the same time as more ordinary food and other products consumed in descent unit activities represented surplus production.

*Surplus and Reproduction.* I will review a few points raised in previous sections, and extend them.

Certain concrete relationships were immediately reproduced in the work process itself and in the everyday sharing of products. Certain other concrete relationships were not. For the Banabans and the other Gilbertese-speaking peoples, these other relationships included ones with "more distant kin," who *(inter alia)* had residual rights to their kinsmen's land, (on some islands) certain use-rights to that land, and (on all islands) use-rights to their kinsmen's productive capacity.

On Banaba many of these people related to one another in

specific contexts "created" by the Banaban descent system—a system of linked bilateral descent units which functioned as groups on particular occasions. Their operation involved surplus.

That what was going on involved surplus is a feature of the structure as a whole: It was surplus vis-à-vis the labor process and the everyday consumption requirements of the producers and their dependents, and surplus vis-à-vis the everyday consumption requirements of people who were producing or had produced for them in everyday life—especially their parents and grandparents. Structurally it "had" to be surplus, as the reproduction of concrete relationships here was focussed on reproduction which did not occur in the same sense in the labor process and in the everyday sharing of products. Yet the relationships reproduced through the descent system, and in other circumstances between more distant kin, were implicated in the reproduction of relationships involved in the labor process and in the sharing of products. They were implicated in the specific sense of reproduction into the next generation (through marriage and the procreation of children; through the transmission of rights to heritable property). And it is in this reproduction into the next generation—certainly for the Banabans, and to different degrees for the peoples of other Gilbertese-speaking islands—that the bilateral character of the system is revealed, as links through men *and* women mattered very much.

One of the things that the descent system was, was an internal link between the production of socialized surplus and the reproduction of relationships.

It is important here to recall a point made early in the chapter: relationships were construed as being real. And as relationships they were not merely relations between persons, but included aspects of persons, their behavior and property to which they had rights. Hence their "reproduction" had to have its more literal moments. As part of their reproduction, for the instance of the descent system, persons (directly or through their delegates and products), ways of behaving, products and property were simultaneously present in specialized contexts—as they were also co-present in the day-to-day reproduction of relations involved in the labor process and the sharing of products.

For the feasts and activities related to them which are charac-

teristic of the peoples of these islands, it is easy to see how prestige could derive from producing much for the purpose and
contributing it: as reproduction had its more literal moments (at
least in my interpretation), perhaps contributing more had the
consequence of making that reproduction stronger, more intense.

## PRODUCTION AND COUNTER-PRODUCTION

We can tentatively identify relations between ownership and
supervision which differ from capitalist production relations.
For the Gilbertese-speaking peoples as reported in the source
ethnographies, we find: (a) supervision of productive capacity
which occurs between elder and junior "gender-mates," as part
of a process in time and within relationships, where the elders
transmit property (e.g., skills, special knowledge) to the juniors,
property which is linked to the activity under supervision, and the
juniors in turn engage in supervision; (b) supervision of productive
capacity which occurs within and across gender, also part of a process in time and within relationships, where the elders transmit
property (e.g., land, prerogatives) to juniors, property which is
also linked to the activity being supervised; juniors in turn engage
in supervision; (c) supervision of productive capacity which occurs
across gender (particularly men vis-à-vis women), tied to property
owned within gender (e.g., in the reconstruction: the *kouti* and
related "ritual" practices, if they were men's property which
men were using for positive consequences for women as well as
for themselves).

We can incorporate the foregoing into a global orientation
toward Banaban and Gilbertese societies in terms of productive
capacity, supervision, ownership, cooperation and use-right, including ownership and supervision of what people produce and
the increment realized on what they own or produce (cf. Sahlins
1972:chapter 4, Godelier 1977:chapters 4, 5 and 9).

Such an orientation allows us to place into perspective a number of practices which were believed to have the consequence of
interrupting production and reproduction. Phrased otherwise:
as people had capacities which advanced production and reproduction, they also had capacities which could interrupt—or did interrupt—the "orderly process." Analytically, we can see the exercise

of such "capacities" as posing threats to the reproduction of the relations of production; the response to such threats was by separating the threatening people (in different ways) from what they were threatening, by withdrawing them from production. The ideological-practical aspects of "counter-production" seem dialectically related to the ideological-practical aspects of "production," suggesting that, in this cultural setting, the productivity-fertility-growth themes and metaphors had an internally related negative side. The suggestion is reinforced by another one: that on the counter-production side women tended to be identified as the "guilty party" (cf. Buchbinder and Rappaport 1976, Godelier 1977:chapter 9), as in many matters between men and women, men supervised their combination while women supervised their separation. Instances of this aspect of women's position emerge below. [62]

*Sex and Food.* We are presented with special problems by what appears to have been a pattern of sexual intercourse not combining very well with a number of other things. One cannot say too much as the available ethnography is limited. But it does seem to have been the case that sexual intercourse was especially separated from what each gender did on its own, the development of which was supervised by same-gender elders. What men and women did in combination sexually had a negative effect on what they did separately. (Since contact between genders—including procreative contact—was necessary for what each gender did to realize its use-value, we encounter the paradoxical position of sexuality familiar from the Melanesian literature.)

Consider the following examples:

(1) Men and the *kouti* ritual: the Maudes observed that Banaban men had to abstain from sexual intercourse for a year if they were trying to become expert in the more physically arduous forms of the *kouti* ritual. Such men would live on the terraces (Maude and Maude 1932:282-283). I suggest here that there were two (internally related) aspects to this practice: staying away from women, and staying away from sex.

(2) Men and fishing: some Banaban and Gilbertese men today say that men should abstain from sexual intercourse the night before fishing. There is also a female side: while men are fishing, women in their households should ensure that no one steps on the

men's sleeping mats; otherwise, the fish might fall from the hooks. Perhaps women could be blamed for unsuccessful fishing.

(3) Women and cooking: Grimble recounts an incident from Tarawa, from which he learned that love-making had to be kept out of the cookhouse. A woman's daughter and the daughter's lover were sleeping together in the mother's cookhouse. The spirits of the earth oven engendered poisonous winds which entered the food being cooked, sickening the woman's husband and father who were living with her. The husband and father thrashed the woman on the morning of the incident (Grimble 1957:131-136). Here the question is not one of male or female abstinence, but of keeping sex out of the kitchen, the woman's kitchen.

(4) Women and tattooing: Grimble recounts his tattooing by a man of a clan associated with the sun, in the Gilberts. Two of the man's granddaughters acted as assistants, to comfort Grimble. The general practice was for girls to comfort the person undergoing the tattooing. A girl doing this had to be a virgin. The tattooer said: "No woman who has known a man has power to do this thing, for the comfort has gone out of her. Nor would any not a virgin dare to offer herself for the task. If she did, the sun would pierce her navel with all the pain of the tattooing, and she would die" (Grimble 1932:226). The virgin girl had some sort of capacity as a conduit, which capacity no longer existed if she had engaged in sexual relations. Here women who were not yet fully adult women, who were still being supervised by elder women, had a special power of which men could in fact take special advantage.

(5) Men and women and procreation: recall that according to Grimble, women "lay apart" from their husbands between pregnancy and childbirth (while women's sisters may have provided sexual consolation), during which period pregnant women were being looked after by other women. At least on some islands there was also a post-partum sexual taboo on women, and there were food and related taboos and recommendations which applied to pregnant or nursing women.

Eating prohibited foodstuffs would negatively affect the child, in at least one case through the mother's milk, imparting undesirable qualities of body or character. For example, cowardice could be induced by contact with turtle (because it crawled); misshapen hands and incestuous tendencies could be induced by contact with the remnants of fish used as bait (the fish had a hacked appearance, and had been in "close union" with its sibling, the hook). [63] If a pregnant woman ate something forbidden to her husband or brother, the child could suffer the consequences (Grimble 1933-1934:21-22, 36). There is no record of foods being forbidden to the husband or brother of the pregnant woman. While others presumably had to take care not to give these things to pregnant or nursing women, we can assume that these women had to take care themselves not to eat them; perhaps they could be blamed if something was wrong with the child.

On the positive side, there were things which were especially good for pregnant women to eat. The land crab was the best, for a good supply of milk. On Banaba, the land crab is the embodiment of a male spirit. Among other things were fish (ibid.:34), and men were fishermen.

We can thus discern prohibitions separating sexual intercourse from other productive acts, the violation of which interfered with productivity. We can also discern prohibitions where women had conceived—where, making certain assumptions about precolonial theories of procreation—women had produced sexual-procreative substance which was being transmitted to the next generation. We can also discern prohibitions about the time when women produced substance which was *not* being transmitted to the next generation: the menstrual taboo. Violating the first interfered with the productivity of each gender; violating the second interfered with the production of the child: violating the third interfered with production in general.

*The Menstrual Taboo.* Menstruation was an unproductive activity in which women had to engage but which men did not control. The menstrual taboo was a prohibition on contact between menstruating women and anything that had to do with productivity, and between women and men as men gained access to the source of their strengthening powers. The menstrual taboo withdrew menstruating women from production, and deprived them of their women's rights. To elaborate:

Recall the Banaban terraces and platforms, where men performed *kouti* ritual, tamed frigate birds, engaged in male initiations, and so forth. The Maudes wrote: "The reason why no woman should come near was for fear lest they might be menstruating, a menstruating woman having a lethal effect on magic" (Maude and Maude 1932:282). The magic (or, as I have preferred to term it, ritual) involved was that through which men acquired success and prowess, health and strength, from the sun. The leading descent group in the meeting-house on many islands in the Gilberts, which established its position in the eighteenth century in part through conquest, was also associated with the sun (see Maude 1963).

Now given the fact that the 'houses of menstruation' existed for menstruating women, and that at any time there were many females who, one could have been confident, were not menstruating, the local explanation has to be taken as a very complex statement. There was something about women which was lethal to the male ritual devoted to their acquisition of success and prowess, health and strength, and this was stated (by men and women?) in terms of menstruation.

Menstruation was also linked to separations in eating together. In the general pattern, Grimble observed that members of the household ate together.

> The only persons excluded from the board are women and girls during menstruation. These eat not only apart from the rest, but also if there be two of them, apart from each other. At this period, it is said of a woman that 'she stands outside' *(e tei iao)*, which signifies that, although she may take her meals at the same times as her fellow-householders, she must eat at a distance from the main communal dwelling. In fair weather, she occupies a mat on the ground a few yards from the house; at other times, she may eat in some outhouse, provided that she takes care not to touch any agricultural or domestic implement in the neighbourhood. She uses special eating and drinking vessels, which may not be brought into the dwelling, and are carefully washed in sea-water and stowed away in a secret place after each meal. On the fourth day after complete cessation of the flow, the woman wraps all utensils in the mat upon which she has sat, and returns to the household board (Grimble 1933-1934:43).

In the 'houses of menstruation' on Banaba, the food, dishes and sleeping mats used by menstruating women were used by them only, and they also bathed from a separate part of the reef.[84]

Grimble also observed that menstruating women could not

touch food or instruments related to food, with the exception of things which the women needed for their own meals. Pregnant or nursing mothers did not have to engage in a number of work activities, but they were not prohibited from doing so (ibid.:5).

Cooking food, serving food and engaging in certain horticultural activities were aspects of women's productive capacity. By being prohibited from engaging in horticulture, and from cooking food for others and serving food to others, menstruating women were being deprived of their rights as women.

If menstruating women could cause so much trouble, it is reasonable for us to think that they had a great deal of "power." I have eschewed the use of the term power here because I do not know what precolonial power-like concepts were. We can at least say that menstruating women were in a state which had great consequences for the life activity of other people. If we use the looser term powers, we can formulate part of the issue as follows: menstruating women had powers which were inimical to the attainment of powers by men.

The ethnography suggests that through ritual, men had to attain their powers from the sun. Women learned things from other women, including knowledge (powers?) relating to what Grimble termed "lovemaking." But we might regard the powers tied up with menstruation as powers which were ascribed to their femaleness, powers with which they were thought to be naturally endowed.

As an activity in which women had to engage, which did not represent a combination with men to create a useful product, menstruation was especially lethal to that male activity in which men engaged, out of combination with women, which was useful productively: the *kouti* magic. Or, women's powers uncontrolled by men negatively affected men's access to the source of men's powers. For men to be worried about this sort of thing appears both logical and realistic, and women may have had an interest in it, of one kind or another.

The point can be carried further in another way: Friedl (1975: 29) has suggested that in certain populations, menstruation implied infertility, and as such was negative. This may have been possible among the Banabans. Yet there are some accounts from older Banabans today which suggest that there was a deliberate limitation on population, rather than an emphasis on procreating as much as possible. Conception and birth were not always unalloyed joys for either gender.

I would like to suggest a variant on the infertility interpretation, which joins with the point just made about the necessity of menstruation but men's non-role in it: menstrual blood was a female sexual-procreative substance which was not being transmitted to the next generation through conception. Clearly many assumptions about precolonial theories of procreation are being made, but the idea is a simple one: women had sexual-procreative substance which was not transmitted. The substance in the process of being transmitted advanced production, in combination with men. The substance not in the process of being transmitted interrupted production, out of combination with men. [65]

Accepting the Maudes' observation as a statement of the local explanation as to why women had to be excluded from the terraces and platforms (for fear that a woman might be menstruating, and a menstruating woman has a lethal effect on magic), we can amplify it slightly as: because as part of their femaleness, women's capacity included the necessary capacity to menstruate; but menstruation was unproductive and was the negation of production in general, and of men in particular (cf. Labby 1976a: chapter 5).

The act of menstruation thus actualized a female capacity. As such, it made sense for people to say that women had to be excluded for fear that they were menstruating. And it also made sense to separate menstruating women and to deprive them of their rights as women, to localize them and the problem, while dividing women from one another.

The ethnography from the Gilberts suggests that sexual intercourse was considered weakening, and that men were expected to be rather lecherous. There is an obvious link between the idea of men being weakened by sexual intercourse, and what may have been a male monopoly of access to certain strengthening powers: through the *kouti* ritual, adult men may have partially replenished aspects of their capacities consumed as they interacted with adult women. At least on some Gilbertese islands these powers were also linked to a descent group which, among other things, supervised meeting house activities (the activities involved surplus) since it established its position in the eighteenth century. [66]

*The Incest Taboo Again.* "Treatment" by literal separation or withdrawal from production also occurs with incest, and the sun makes another appearance as an element of the sanction. According to Grimble, an incestuous couple in the Gilberts had to be killed or sent away on the ocean under conditions which almost guaranteed death. Associated with a narrative, the "... belief was that the sun would hide his face from the place in which two such offenders were allowed to live unpunished" (Grimble 1921: 21). If the child was the exemplary new product and the production of children was the exemplary (if not always desirable) production, then both menstruation and incest were interruptions in this production which could negatively affect production in general and which had to be separated from it.

*Reflection on These Taboos.* Perhaps we can make further sense out of a certain unity discernible among menstruation, sexual intercourse and incest.

First, as we have said, they could have counter-productive consequences.

Second, they involved losses (a familiar theme from Melanesia) which were not at the same time preservation or reproduction. Menstruation was a loss; nothing was being preserved or reproduced through new production. During sexual intercourse, particularly for men, something was lost and whether or not there was going to be new production (a child) remained to be seen. Incest was sexual activity of course, and furthermore the resulting child would not be new production.

Third, the menstrual taboo, the incest taboo and the prohibition on combining sexual intercourse with other productive activities represented separations in people's relations to their activities, to their products and to other people. The menstrual taboo made men and women non-substitutable for one another. The incest taboo made particular men non-substitutable for other particular men in relation to women, and made particular women non-substitutable for particular women, in relation to men. The restrictions on combining sexual intercourse with other activities made sexual intercourse non-substitutable for other productive activities. The menstrual taboo separated what women were and did into that part which included male action and was fresh production, and that part which did not include male action, was not fresh production, and was negative for production. The incest taboo separated production that was not fresh production from production that was fresh production, by separating people's sexuality from themselves and from one another in the first instance, and uniting their sexuality with themselves and with one another in the second.

And fourth, menstruation, sexual intercourse and incest were actual or potential failures of control, threats to the relations of production, at the same time as sexual intercourse and at least first menstruation were necessary for the relations of production to be reproduced. Hence, threats to the relations of production, the separations which constitute those relations, counter-productive consequences, and non-preserving and non-reproducing losses become part of the same system of relations. [67]

CONCLUSION

This chapter *is* a set of very speculative conclusions, from a restricted corpus of reports which I have attempted to study closely. Hence I will not restate the points developed in the argument. Since the account has been a basically static one, I might call attention to two ways in which the "re-embedding" of the material dealt with in the account could be made: looking to the precolonial past and to the colonial past.

Looking to the precolonial past, we clearly need more interpretation as well as data on the historical relations among peoples in the area (especially in the light of Luomala 1974), warfare, trade, and "ecological" factors such as droughts and soil conditions on the different islands (Catala 1957). While some of the developments toward greater stratification in the Northern and Central Gilberts were tied to the colonial era, not all of those developments were, and one would want to be able to "think" more systematically the implications of the absence on Banaba of conditions favorable to the growth of the large taro, and their presence in the Gilberts. The Banaban and Gilbertese ethnographies may inform each other in this regard. I am not suggesting an ecological or technological determinism. What these peoples did is as much a product of their acting on their own situation as it is a product of anything else. At the same time it would be foolish not to explore in detail the differences between people's relations to their land and water which might relate to the availability or nonavailability of particular things which could become means of production used for consumption and reproduction. Perhaps we can re-open Sahlins' argument in a new light (Sahlins 1958; cf. Godelier 1977).[68]

Looking to the colonial past, if the argument on socialized surplus holds water, perhaps we can gain insight into one of the ways in which many of these people have been able to sustain important aspects of their culture in spite of the inroads of colonialism. If the nature of their "social whole" were such that a radical change in any one aspect would bring the rest down, they would not be who they are today.

As far as the Banabans were concerned, before phosphate mining began at the turn of the century they articulated with colonialism most clearly through some trade (probably not on a large scale; petty commodity production) and then, in addition, the Protestant church. With small-scale trade the reproduction of pre-colonial relations of production could occur as the control of property and labor processes was still in the people's hands. I have interpreted the early activities of the Protestant church as coming to "occupy" the higher levels of the descent system, both in terms of where the church buildings were, and the kinds of activities in which the religious groups engaged (Silverman 1971: chapter 3). By 1900, a male missionary and a male phosphate company official had even been taken into the water-caves—but by Banaban women.

Involvement in the church had important consequences for the community, yet many Banabans attended it erratically in the early period and pre-colonial ritual activities have been revivified in particular political-economic contexts since (see Silverman 1971). Perhaps in the early colonial period, both in the sale of goods and involvement in the foreign religion, the people were being "penetrated" first in those aspects of their own social formation which were most immediately tied up with what I have hypothesized here can be seen in terms of "socialized surplus" in some way. At that point, and in that special way, their history and our own history, their relations of production and our own, became linked. The situation escalated when the colonial government *de facto* asserted control over their lands. By this point the Banabans had been moving more and more in the direction of community activism and autonomy, in relations with outside forces. When the phosphate company wanted more Banaban land to mine in 1927 there were an important number of hold-outs among the people. In 1928 the colonial government passed an ordinance which gave it the power to settle the issue if negotiations failed. The government arranged an "arbitration," and the modern era of Banaban colonial history began.

# NOTES

## Chapter 1. Impasses in Social Theory

1. We would like to thank Vern Carroll and JoAnn Magdoff for helpful comments on a draft of this chapter.
2. We will take up the critique of Foucault's work elsewhere.
3. See, e.g., Buchbinder and Rappaport 1976, Goldman 1970:448 et seq., Rappaport 1967, Sahlins 1972:149-183.
4. Some of these matters are discussed in a variety of recent publications, e.g., Hymes, ed., 1972; Jarvie 1975.
5. The issue is of course not a new one; see Stocking 1974.
6. For a very interesting discussion of contrasting ways of using categories, see Steiner 1967 [1956], chapter 1.
7. Some examples: on complexity, see Bellah 1964, Parsons 1966; on embeddedness, see Dalton 1965; on kinship relations as infrastructure and superstructure, see Godelier 1972 (cf. Terray 1972).
8. The most thorough-going critique of a category is D.M. Schneider's discussion of kinship; see, e.g., Schneider 1968, 1972. For questions on the incest taboo, see Needham 1971b; for questions on marriage, see Rivière 1971. Works spelling out the other kind of position include H. Schneider 1975; Swartz, Turner and Tuden 1966.
9. We have in mind aspects of Althusser 1969:213 et seq.; Godelier 1972:98 et seq., 259; cf. Terray 1972:149 et seq., Dumont 1970:231-234.
10. The recent work of Raymond Williams stands out in this regard. For an indication of the complexities involved in assessing the general applicability of categories which emerge most clearly under capitalism, see Marx's discussion of abstract labor, Marx 1967 [1867]:59-60. For a discussion of changing conceptions of symbols, see Foucault 1973 [1966].
11. See Whorf on the relationship between the form of accounting and the form of time-reckoning in the West, Whorf 1956 [1941]; Lee on lineality and the self, Lee 1959 [1950].
12. It is interesting to see the call for a retreat from the more familiar types of comprehensive theory by figures as diverse as Murdock (1972) and Needham (1971a).
13. We refer here to certain tendencies in approaches stressing "interpretation" or hermeneutics.
14. Wagner deals with some similar things in his recent book; see Wagner 1975. See Ewen 1976 for a preliminary discussion of the development of the advertising industry.
15. See discussion in Lane 1964.
16. For more discussion see Sebag 1964.
17. There are important issues raised here related to recent discussions in the philosophy of science. See especially the articles by Kuhn, Popper and Feyerabend in Lakatos and Musgrave 1970.
18. See Althusser and Balibar 1970.
19. Consider Althusser's "subject;" Althusser 1971.
20. See, e.g., the organization of chapter headings in Edwards, Reich and Weisskopf 1972.
21. See the treatment of superstructure in Nikitin 1966.
22. We have in mind pamphlets and other publications of the CPUSA on racism and

sexism.

23. See, e.g., Goldmann 1973-1974, and other articles in *Telos*.

24. The concepts of metaphor and metonymy are much discussed in the recent structuralist literature, much of it drawing on Lévi-Strauss 1966. A recent salvo on the question of "extensions" is Scheffler and Lounsbury 1971; cf. Schneider 1968.

25. See, e.g., Godelier 1974, Habermas 1975; for orthodox marxism, see, e.g., Cornforth 1952-1954.

26. See discussion in Lefebvre 1971.

27. Consider, e.g., Poulantzas 1973.

## Chapter 2. Separations in Capitalist Societies:
### Persons, Things, Units and Relations

1. We would like to thank Vern Carroll, Carole Farber, JoAnn Magdoff and David Schneider for helpful comments on an earlier draft of this chapter.

2. There is an interesting discussion of Maine in Burrow 1966.

3. Other places in which such contrasts were raised, with links to the study of domination, include Mauss 1970 [1925], Simmel (see Wolff, ed., 1964), and Polanyi 1944.

4. The uncritical study of "modernization" and "development" is increasingly challenged as the links between the more naive kind of positivist epistemology and the justification of Cold War positions become more apparent.

5. An essential feature of a certain construction of contract is underscored by Pierre E. Trudeau: "It is... a fundamental axiom, though it is often not recognized as such, that every system of contract law as a provider of justice is based on the assumption of equality of status of the two parties to the contract: [footnote omitted] without this equality, justice—if indeed there is any justice present—*never* proceeds from the contract" (Trudeau 1974 [1956] :336). We recognize that the notion and practice of contract has undergone significant changes over time, and is not the same in all places, but we cannot pursue that theme here.

6. An important literature exists on the issue of the interpretation of housework. See, e.g., Meissner, Humphreys, Meis and Scheu 1975; Rowbotham 1973. Rowbotham also explores the question of "separations," which is a focus of our volume.

7. Engels dealt precisely with this issue; see Engels 1968 [1884] :505-507. See also Goldmann 1973.

8. "Substantive" might be a more felicitous term, but it has been pre-empted, in making a logically related point, by Weber. See Weber 1968.

9. Meillassoux observed: "More consideration should be given to the distinction between status and contract societies made by early social scientists such as Maine, Morgan or Toennies, in order to understand the qualitative change undertaken by our present society in relation to the feudal one" (Meillassoux 1972: 104, footnote 3). This observation (see Marx 1967 [1867] :76 et seq.) sparked much of the organization of the present argument. In his paper, Meillassoux (following Marx) speaks of a "... state of social, *personal* dependency" in "...kinship or feudal society" (ibid.:95). Without raising the question of the adequacy

of those terms for other societies, we find the personal/abstracted domination contrast useful for capitalist ideology. See also Bernstein 1972.

10. Weber himself wrote of *Herrschaft* and *legitime Herrschaft.* In his translation, Parsons (see Weber 1964 [1947]) finds words such as authority and imperative coordination to be more congenial. See Cohen, Hazelrigg and Pope 1975.

11. Problems in this area are discussed by Rowbotham 1973, Smith 1973.

12. "Responsibility" is brought up in Firth, Hubert and Forge 1969, a work with which we have just become familiar. At some point a full comparison of the American and British studies would be very helpful. Firth, Hubert and Forge give central and detailed attention to the relation between "... generalized, fairly standardized canons of responsibility toward kin... ."(ibid.:451), choice and the specifics of situations in which the stance toward the content of particular responsibilities (which may be a matter of ambiguity and conflict) emerges as a product of how other kin carry out their responsibilities. The British presentation suggests a more "contractual tinge" to many relations than does the American material, but at the same time the diffuseness of the standards, their often moral quality, and the special quality of blood relations, are noted. While there does seem to be more of a contractual tinge: "Obligations and responsibilities have to be assessed in the light of personal judgment, not formal rule. Claims are made, expectations are presented, duties conceived, with no clear guide for their resolution in action. Much of the peculiar quality of kinship lies in this" (ibid.: 453). Comparison with studies of kinship among working class people becomes of particular interest.

13. During a discussion of Schneider 1968 in an anthropology seminar (University of Western Ontario 1975), E. Durrant asked whether Schneider's "pure domains" (e.g., of kinship, sex) could really be seen as such. The question can be appropriated as follows: can one consider, say, the relation between husband and wife independently of domination? Is that sexuality which "unites what is different" not part and parcel of the same thing as that sexuality which dominates? This is an issue dealt with by a variety of critically and clinically oriented scholars.

14. During a discussion of Dumont's work on individualism in an anthropology seminar (University of Western Ontario 1975), P. Jensen observed that his approach did not deal with differences between men and women. That observation sparked much more thought about Dumont's points.

15. We are indebted to M.R. Barnett for this observation.

16. And the bonds in which corporations are involved include bonds which could appear diffuse; the Morgan Bank, for example, was far more influential than its actual holdings would suggest; see, e.g., Lundberg 1968.

17. This is clearly an aspect of the "structure-in-dominance" in a sense related to Althusser's; see Althusser 1969, Althusser and Balibar 1970.

18. This may situate V. Turner's concept of "liminality" as ideological.

19. One has in mind here aspects of game theory, decision-making theory, value theory à la Kenneth Arrow.

20. On structure-in-dominance, see Althusser 1969, Althusser and Balibar 1970.

21. One of the more visible instances of the paradox is the voters' paradox. Here the claims of the substantialized individual are in conflict with those of the contractualized group.

22. Speaking of women in upper middle class families under corporate capitalism, where the woman's activities are directed toward sustaining an imaged order, Smith writes:

At the same time the service the woman gives in the home is trivialized. It is no longer a service essential to the creation of minimal comfort and security. First, affluence diminishes what goes into the maintenance of a household order in the ability to purchase services and equipment. Secondly, there is a transfer to skill from the individual to the technology both in the development of household machines and in the processing of food and clothes, etc. Thus skills previously essential to and recognizable in, the production of food, of clothes, repairs, etc., are appropriated by the manufacturing process. The corporate enterprise mediates between the raw and the cooked (Smith 1973: 24-25).

We must recognize this and the fact that the continuing reproduction of some "pre-capitalist" forms of organization is good for capitalism (see Meillassoux 1972:101-102).

23. We are reading Marx's idea of the person not as the prior autonomous unit of all social forms, but as a development of capitalist forms of production, a unit created through a specific type of exchange with the fact of exchange in society being prior. Thus rather than the person's interaction with nature being the foundation of society, forms of interaction within society create the person as a moral agent. We therefore do not assume the stance that the goal of the communist society of Marx is the liberation of the individual, presented in terms of substance and code, but rather an overcoming of the problematic of present individualist ideology.

24. This is a general formulation and is not, of course, intended to equate, say, European feudalism and caste hierarchy in pre-capitalist India.

25. Given the relations set out between (1) use-value and exchange-value, and (2) substance-enactment, contract-performance, an obvious next analytic step is clearly to explore their relations with the meta-language of meaning. Consider, for example, the idea of the "natural symbol" in which meaning appears to inhere in the symbol itself, as opposed to the "arbitrary" or "external" relation between signifier and signified in which the signified appears to be determined in its contrast to other signifieds (or significata). Consider also the attention to meaning in (reified) context, as opposed to meaning in the context of more abstract systems. In many approaches, the manner of handling the construction of meaning does not immediately come to theoretical terms with the relations of production. Those relations may even be mystified or ignored, as is the case with commodities: that is, relations between people can be mystified as relations between things, and as relations between symbols or concepts or contexts, which at the meta-level (or in "theoretical practice") appear as meta-things (or as theoretical things, abstractions). We are thus anthropologically confronted with the issue of that unity to the mystification of the relations of production which Marx outlined. And we are epistemologically confronted with the issue of whether it is possible for us as analysts to systematically construct the "options" in any other way. If we know whether we can answer this question, we will have answered the question itself. Gödel lives in anthropology, in the question of the relation between the framing of analytic options and the options themselves.

It may seem as though there are naturally only certain ways in which things can be interrelated. For example, that they can be continuous with one another or separated from one another; that they can be internal to one another or external to one another. On this line of reasoning, Marx's contrasts could be seen as operating within the universe of such natural distinctions.

However, we would hypothesize that notions akin to our notions of inside-ness and outsideness, internality and externality, are themselves not universal, and that differences in such notions relate to differences in the organization of production. And further, that if one considers matters in this way, new approaches to old conundrums emerge, and we escape from the dilemmas of anthropological butterfly collecting (in Leach's phrase; Leach 1961), and the dilemmas which make us pose notions such as "mystical participation."

26. Of course, this should not be read as suggesting a simple return to holism, a relinking of substance and code. Caste or feudal society is not exactly an inspiring vision for the future. We are only indicating that the individual as substance and code cannot be the basis for "unalienated man."

## Chapter 3. Gender and Separations in Precolonial Banaban and Gilbertese Societies

1. In this chapter I am covering some of the same analytic territory in Oceania as a number of current works, e.g., Buchbinder and Rappaport 1976 (although we begin from different directions). Weiner kindly sent me a few pre-publication chapters of Weiner 1976 which were very helpful. Comments by Goodale at an Association for Social Anthropology in Oceania workshop on gender roles were also very thought-provoking. I would like to thank Steve Barnett, Vern Carroll, Carole Farber and David Schneider for comments on a draft of this chapter. Jim Lindsey and Ian Parnell were helpful with references.

2. See, e.g., Burridge 1958, Damon 1978, Hogbin 1970, Labby 1976a, Rappaport 1967, Schieffelin 1976, Silverman 1971, Weiner 1976.

3. In writing of the Northern Gilberts, Lambert (1941:147) uses a distinction between "real" and "personal" property, real property primarily being land, taro gardens and large canoes; he points out that people have access to real property because of their status as members of groups. The situation on Banaba cannot be described in so straightforward a manner.

4. A number of recent works, particularly about societies in the Melanesian area, deal with gender, e.g., Goodale and Chowning 1971, Kõngãs-Maranda 1974, Strathern 1972, Weiner 1976.

5. For example, in a paper which I had received but, unfortunately, did not read closely until most of my text was completed, Strathern writes that the Hagen male/female contrast emphasized "... different spheres of action, different capacities" (Strathern MS.:16).

6. In his brilliant analysis, Kirsch speaks of "fertility" and "potency," concepts which I take to be within the same area as the productive capacity I talk about here. Part of Kirsch's discussion is an argument with Leach about the primacy of religious factors (which Kirsch emphasizes) over political factors (which Leach emphasizes). One might suggest that those terms, as terms of an argument, create as many difficulties as they solve. Much of the spectrum of organization described by Kirsch and Leach may have been present in Oceania.

7. I realize that I am touching on an area of much discussion and controversy in the neomarxist literature—e.g., on the precise delineation of the relations between cooperation, the functions of ownership and control, the relations of production, the forces of production, and the general concepts of mode of production and

social formation. I feel it would be premature to extend the discussion in this chapter further than I have extended it already, since more thought is necessary particularly on the relation between ownership and supervision. This question can only be developed in a dialectical relation with more comparative ethnography.

8. The interpretation of "surplus" within the neomarxist problematic is a complex issue. While there are many inaccuracies regarding precapitalist formations, useful points are made in Mandel 1970. In anticipation of material to be presented later in the chapter, I might note at this point that "surplus" does not necessarily connote "unnecessary," and that in thinking out the question of surplus for precapitalist formations, quantitative questions (how much is produced?) should not overshadow qualitative questions (cf. Damon 1978). The quality of what is produced may be of great concern to the producers. The quantitative issue re-emerges through asking about the amount of time necessary to produce surplus goods which are regarded as being of the necessary quality. This issue in turn raises that of the relations of production which enable that time to be used for that purpose.

9. In most cases where I discuss the meanings of Gilbertese words, the Gilbertese words themselves will be found in a note at the end of a sentence, sub-section or section of the chapter. Glosses given in the notes include only the meanings referred to in the body of the chapter; to include more, I would have to occupy many more pages with the analysis of particular words.

10. Other details of the gender organization of production should be clear through Koch 1965, which I have not had the opportunity to study. The best available description for the Northern Gilberts is Lambert's excellent account (Lambert 1963 and subsequent publications). While I am not dealing specifically with the Northern Gilberts, I am trying to establish a framework to discuss important differences between Banaba, the Southern Gilberts (which in their organization appear closer to the Banaban pattern), and the Northern and Central Gilberts. (Indeed, it is the comparative problem which makes the issue of surplus nearly inescapable.) Butaritari and Makin in the North can be thought of as more highly "stratified" than either Banaba or the Southern islands. A number of Lambert's points make me think that discussion of the Northern Gilberts can proceed in some of the same terms as are being developed here. For example: the major personages having to do with the chieftainship and succession were men rather than women; there was a tendency toward status-level endogamy, one aspect of which was that "... the High Chief's children usually married their first cousins, and his grandchildren, their second cousins" (Lambert 1963:207); there were specific rights and obligations of the chiefly family, aristocrats and commoners with respect to land and its products and in regard to redistribution; the "... fear of the supernatural sanction" of the High Chief was important (ibid.:193, 229); the "... High Chief, his siblings and his children were exempt from productive labor" (ibid.:209), but could work if they wanted to; the Butaritari aristocrats were partially exempt "... from the routine tasks of subsistence" which may have "allowed them more time to make weapons and ornaments, train for war, and carry on ritual activities—memories are now vague on this subject" (ibid.: 251-252). An observation of Lambert's is particularly relevant to the suggestion that there are similarities with the order of problems discussed by Kirsch (1973):

> The powers of the High Chief to settle conflicts and to regulate social relations generally were based mainly on the fear of supernatural sanction if he

were offended and were exercised irregularly. The council of the village Elders seem, on the other hand, to have possessed considerable authority over the actions of the people of their communities; unfortunately, only a few details of their activities are now remembered. The relative importance of the High Chief's office, as Stevenson puts it, was measured by the man. A strong personality might wield almost absolute power in his lifetime, while a weak one would be virtually a puppet in the hands of influential elders [Stevenson 1905:251] (Lambert 1963:193-194).

11. The terms are: *mane* 'man, male', *aine* 'woman, female'; *te mane* 'a man, a male', *te aine* 'a woman, a female'; *te iteranimane* 'the man's/male side', *te iteranaine* 'the woman's/female side'; *te kanoanimane* 'the descendants of the man', *te kanoanaine* 'the descendants of the woman'.

12. Maude writes of the titles: "Ten, or its euphonic variations Tem or Teng (Te in the Northern Gilberts and Na, Nan, Nam or Nang on Butaritari and Little Makin) is the prefix for males and Nei for females" (Maude 1963:10, footnote 15). The definite/indefinite article is *te*.

13. Productive life cycle terms discussed include: *te merimeri* 'the baby', *te tei* 'the youth'; *te kara* 'the aged'; *te teinimane* (or *ataeinimane*) 'the male youngster', *te ataeinaine* 'the female youngster', *te teinaine* 'the female youngster, virgin' (see Lundsgaarde 1966:99); *te unimane* 'the old man', *te unaine* 'the old woman'; *te otaba* 'the adult married woman'; *te nikiranroro* 'the remainder of the generation'; *te rorobuaka* 'the active adult male, member of the warrior generation, member of the fighting generation'; *te roronga* 'the bachelor'; *te nikiranroronga* 'the remainder of the bachelors' (adapted from Lundsgaarde 1966, Sabatier 1954, and my own research).

14. These sex-related terms are: *ana buakaka te mane* 'the man's badness, impurity', *ana buakaka te aine* 'the woman's badness, impurity'; *te moantia* 'transverse part of abdomen under navel, between hips'; *te tinou* 'part immediately above sexual organs'; *te tari* 'liquid, juice'.

15. The terms are: *manena* 'his sexual parts', *ainena* 'her interior reproductive organs'.

16. I cannot, alas, go into detail about terms for the act of sexual intercourse. There is a variety of terms, of different degrees of specificity and generality, including euphemisms.

17. The words referred to in the preceding paragraph are: *mange* 'testicles, male sexual parts, detritus', *ki* 'anus, backside'.

18. See Webster 1866:41, 47; Walkup, "Gilbert Islands Report 1883-85," August 1885, American Board of Commissioners for Foreign Missions, Micronesia Mission, Volume 6; Walkup to Forbes, January 1886, American Board of Commissioners for Foreign Missions, Micronesia Mission, Volume 7; in collection of Houghton Library, Harvard University.

19. *Be* 'skirt, unpleasant'. In Bingham's entries, the male terms to which I refer are *bainimane* and (verbal) *bainimanea* (Bingham 1953 [1908]:59). The female terms are *bainaine* and (verbal) *bainainea* (ibid.).

20. Many Banabans say that Banaba was sometimes referred to as *te aban aine* 'the women's land', because the people were of a peace-loving nature (particularly in contrast to some Gilbertese).

21. I am paraphrasing extensively from Maude and Maude 1932.

22. The 'house of menstruation' was called *te uman teinako: te uman* 'the house of', *teinako* 'menstruation' (using Sabatier's gloss of *teinako*, Sabatier 1954:844); *teinako* has a literal meaning of 'to be placed badly', and perhaps 'to be posi-

tioned away'. In the Maude Papers (Collection of H.E. Maude, Canberra, Australia) it is noted that a "sacred" part of another house could be used; the word 'sacred' *(tabu)* can also mean 'forbidden'.

23. My use of hedging quotation marks around "material" derives from the existence of unanswered questions about the structure of the meaning range of Gilbertese *makuri* 'activity, work'. But I should observe that certain activities which in the West might be considered intellectual, spiritual or religious, rather than material, should be included here.

24. There were, however, conventions indicating a certain reserve in the behavior of same-gender affines.

25. Many of the meanings of the suffix *-na* share a feature of 'actively relating toward', and the suffix is used with kin terms to indicate an active relationship or an adoption. Uses of *-na* include uses indicating possession, use or both. Other words referred to are: *bai* 'thing, property', *baina* 'to use, to possess', *kabaibaia* 'to cause someone to be in a state of inheritance'.

26. The male-related terms are *rorobuaka* 'active adult male', *uman roronga* 'young men's house'.

27. Grimble actually writes of the elder as adopting the junior. Grimble was probably translating "adoption" from *tibuna,* which can also mean 'to adopt as grandchild'. The 'guardian' gloss seems more consistent with the situation.

28. The Banaban practice which Grimble describes was similar in that it involved hair cutting, ordeals and relations between male kin. At one point a grandfather or one of the father's brothers swept a staff above the boy's head, striking away the embers of a small fire which the father had kindled on the head. It was a lucky omen if the staff struck the skull, especially if it drew blood (Grimble 1921:41). Luomala (1974:20) discusses related practices oriented to building endurance and the will to work.

29. The ages given in years in the ethnography are of course approximate; they are variable according to different circumstances.

30. Grimble actually refers to an adoptive grandmother; see note 27, above.

31. For the Gilberts, according to Grimble, the grandmother was also the girl's companion when the girl would spend a year or eighteen months in a dark 'bleaching house' to whiten her skin before marriage. The girl could not work in the dark bleaching house, but her grandmother taught her spells, especially those dealing with love, healing and cooking (Grimble 1921:43). Grimble indicates that the Banaban practice was similar except that the girl was often put in the bleaching house before rather than after puberty (ibid.:44). However, discussion of the bleaching house is lacking in the Maudes' paper. In their notes, a Banaban source, probably an elder male in the early 1930s, says that *te ko* (the name for the bleaching house in the Gilberts) was used by both men and women, thus making the matter too confused to carry forward at this point (Maude Papers).

32. Menstruation terms: *e rara* 'she bleeds', *e aoraki* 'she is sick', *te aoraki* 'the sickness'; also see note 22, above.

33. I note that in the modified translation of the informant's statements presented in Silverman 1971:301, I used the English gloss "role" where 'activity' or 'work' would have been more appropriate.

34. Grimble writes of this house as 'the house of men'. The phrase in Gilbertese indicates that this should read 'the house of human beings'.

35. This is one reason why, for the Gilbertese-speaking area in precolonial times, I prefer to speak of men's and women's "productive capacities" rather than men's

and women's "domains" (cf. Weiner 1976). In general, things which we can most clearly identify as isolable had things within them which linked them to what appears as something else which is isolable. Things are not juxtaposed, but inter-related from within. And this is one reason why it is so difficult to construct a neat, linear description, why one can get a sense of a social whole which is a unity of internally related determinations. One of the questions which must be answered so that the whole can be depicted correctly is the nature and scope of precolonial trade (see Luomala 1965:30).

36. It is a common anthropological observation that time in other kinds of forma-tions is not always allocated according to principles of capitalist rationality, but rather includes factors bearing on the cultivation of relationships, solidarity, etc. In this section I am incorporating that insight into the analytic framework being used here.

37. We can thus borrow from "human capital theory" developed in the West!

38. There is an interesting Banaban term, *te kanoanikainga*, which I did not hear used often in everyday circumstances. It can be used for people who marry to the members of a kindred ('in-marrying spouses'). In Gilbertese, *kainga* is (speaking generally) 'hamlet, area' and *kanoa* can be glossed as 'contents' (Silverman 1971: 249). In other usages, *kanoa* can be more narrowly glossed as 'issue' or 'descen-dants' (see note 11, above). As a verb, *kanoa* can mean 'to fill up'. Could the *kanoanikainga*, then, have been those who "filled up the hamlet," through pro-creation?

39. On terms for incest and the meanings of their morphemes, see Eastman 1948: 60; Lundsgaarde 1966:166; Maude 1963:63; Bingham 1953 [1908]:100; Sabatier 1954:366, 389-390, 406, 722-723.

40. Sibling (really "same generation") terms: *tariu* 'my same gender sibling', *maneu* 'my different gender sibling'. The relation between the word for 'different gender sibling' and the word for 'man, male, penis', and the relation between the word for 'same gender sibling' and the word for 'juice, sperm, etc.', is an issue the discussion of which must be postponed until more work on Gilbertese phonology and morphology in historical and comparative (Oceanic) perspective has been conducted. If these relations can be established as semantically live or as ety-mologically real, the analysis could be developed in some rather extraordinary directions.

41. The terms are: *tinau* 'my mother', *tamau* 'my father', *natiu* 'my child', *tibuu* 'my grandperson.' The terms I am using comprise a sort of minimal paradigm, but one cannot unambiguously distinguish a closed set of "kinship terms;" see discussion in Silverman 1971.

42. For relations in generations more distant than grandparent and grandchild, there are reciprocal terms which are not, however, widely used or universally under-stood. The most common I encountered were: "... *tibutoru* for three generations removal; *tibumamano* for four; *tibutaratara* for five. These are, then, marked in relationship to *tibu*. There are some folk etymologies of these terms which ex-plain them by the progressive incapacity of the people in the categories as they ascend" (Silverman 1971:241).

43. I realize that the use of "neutralized" here is a loaded use. On cultural grounds it seems justified.

44. Same generation in-law terms are: *butikau* 'my brother-in-law' (between men), *kainumau* 'my sister-in-law' (between women), *eirikiu* 'my different gender sibling-in-law'. (In the past, the affinal terminology may have been somewhat different; Silverman 1971:259-261). I emphasize the point that reciprocal specific

gender occurs in the context of marriage, as an aspect of the system as a whole: Sexual relations may have been the paradigmatic relations between adult men and women as men and women participating jointly in the same activity. This links to the discussion of the ways in which gender is encoded, in that the gender differences noted are aspects of sexuality and procreation. This point is interesting given the emphasis on the separate development of the productive capacity of each gender and the "polluting" aspects of sexuality. The point as extended links back to the interpretation of the "kin terms" themselves: while everyday usage may vary from the genealogical pattern, as far as reproduction is concerned the genealogical pattern is generally followed.

45. Looking at the islands comparatively, it seems to be a minimal boundary; beyond Banaba the boundary was wider in ancient times, and remains wider in some places.

46. 'Fourth generation' is *kaaroro: roro* 'generation', *a* 'four'. *Ka-* is commonly the causative prefix but in some uses can be interpreted as indicating what seems to be an inchoative, in the sense that something "comes into being." (I thank C. Creider for pointing this out to me.) The inchoative interpretation illuminates the fact that ordinal numbers are formed by prefixing *ka-* to the number morph.

47. See Sabatier 1954:249, entry for *ewe*.

48. *Toru* 'erection'; see note 42, above.

49. The line of argument here thus re-situates and incorporates the use of "identity" and "code" in Silverman 1971.

50. This interpretation is directly informed by Marx's discussion of the quality of living labor in the notes for the chapter on capital in the *Grundrisse*. See Marx 1973 [1857-1858], especially pp. 354-364; cf. Marx 1967 [1867]: chapters 7 and 8. That the argument developed in the *Grundrisse* should be applicable to matters of "kinship" is in retrospect not surprising, as Marx is partially using the language of substances.

51. The analytic language used could be developed to construct an argument on sexuality itself as a "surplus product." Such an argument, however, would be only metaphoric without further data.

52. I am not making a case here for the applicability of a notion of "abstract labor" or even "abstract gender labor." I am rather calling attention to the ethnographic points raised, which require more serious theoretical discussion.

53. See Maude 1963:59-61, and discussions of *tinaba* and *eiriki* relations in other ethnographies of the Gilberts.

54. There are circumstances in which the data could allow one to speak of "exchanges" involving marriage or sexual services and land (see Silverman 1971, Lundsgaarde 1974:208; cf. Labby 1976a, 1976b). Even more directly, we find transactions involving the transfer of land as a kind of payment for "special services rendered," and as compensation for crimes (Maude and Maude 1932). The circumstances generally concerned matters in the more immediate aspects of the "production and reproduction of immediate life" (e.g., land for food in times of drought; and in the Gilberts, land for certain sexual relations between affines). I suggest that the transactions were transactions which the system did not feature as part of the ordinary operations of everyday life. They were "historical," and indeed remarkable.

55. *Kanoan T* 'the issue of T', *te kawa* 'the district, village', *te kainga* 'the hamlet', *kain T* 'the people of T'. See Silverman 1971 for a discussion of the complexities involved in glossing these terms.

56. In the Banaban histories of descent groups, there are instances where an ancestress

was allocated rights to a water-cave, whereas her brother was allocated the right of 'the word' in the descent unit. Lundsgaarde (1966) observed that young women go to the wells to get water in the Southern Gilberts. He also writes of the ownership of *nei* (the same word as the female title?—see note 12, above). A *nei* is:

> A small brackish pond filled with stagnant subsurface water. It is used exclusively by women who use it to soak both pandanus and coir sennit materials employed in the manufacture of mats, thatch, and rope. Ponds owned by two or more women are marked by boundaries. Ownership is transferred to female relatives only. On the southern atolls, *nei* also denotes a large fish pond.... (Lundsgaarde 1974:211-212, footnote 2).

57. Data remain to be acquired on rights in the canoe passages.

58. Given the discussion in the previous chapters, we must try to shed some light on the question of how to think of the descent units as units at all. It is in fact difficult to speak without qualification about units organized into different levels of the system (e.g., hamlets, hamlet coalitions or sub-districts, districts), and to sort activities out as specifically applying to one level rather than to another. One of the reasons for the difficulty is that these "units" were probably in a continuous process of fission and reamalgamation, and of surfacing as important and becoming unimportant. The ethnography from different points in time is not exactly comparable for these reasons. If we speak of any of the units as a unit, we can focus on the persons (or llnes); lands, caves, and foreshores; and prerogatives which it may hold. But immediately as we do this, to preserve any sense of what I take to be the Banaban reality we must simultaneously focus on the unit's relations to other units, and on how the unit is differentiated from within. This is so if we focus on persons or lines, and the simplest example of the point is genealogy. Units are linked genealogically to other units, and the genealogy continues within the unit. This is so if we focus on land; the units were on territories which were part of larger territories, and there were sub-territories within the units. This is so if we think of prerogatives; the prerogatives of one unit existed in relation to the prerogatives of other units, and there were linked prerogatives within the unit. "Unit" itself may thus be a misleading word, and this recalls Dumont's discussion of hierarchy in some ways. A set of interrelated aspects made a unit visible as a unit, linked it with other units and were implicated in the unit's construction from within. We might want to call the units "relational units." As with systems which are more truly segmentary in nature, one must not reify the units as units, think of them as having an existence apart from their "outside relations" and their "inside relations" in the manner of thinking about townships within counties within provinces. The epistemology of the descent system seems to be not that "the whole is greater than the sum of all its parts," but that "the whole is the relations between its parts." (Also see note 35, above.)

59. See Goldman 1970 for an interesting discussion of such principles which embed them in wider issues in Polynesia; Lundsgaarde has discussed such principles for the Gilberts in publications cited.

60. As with use-value and exchange-value, and substantialized and contractualized relations in capitalist ideology, once the separation is made, the separated elements could develop on different but interrelated courses. It is at times of articulated contradiction that the separation becomes most apparent. And in both

cases, ours and theirs, the articulation of contradiction appears as an interruption in the normal course of events. But in our case, and perhaps in theirs also, the possibility of the articulation of contradiction is a precondition of the terms (what is the same, what is different) in which normalcy is itself defined.

61. The "formal deliveries of food" to the Butaritari high chief "acknowledged his ultimate rights to the resources of his islands" (Lambert 1966:161). The commoner ramages included ramages descended from immigrants (ibid.:160; cf. Silverman 1971, Labby 1976a). For Beru, Maude recorded rights of Te Bakoa "as titular owners of the island, to the first-fruits of the pandanus harvest...." (Maude 1963:37). Te Bakoa was the place (in the meeting house) of the descendants of Tabuariki. The descendants of Tabuariki (with others) lived on Beru before the arrival of the group which established the more contemporary meeting house and descent group system (ibid.:10-13). Integrating this data with Banaban accounts—and disputes—about the history of the descent system (discussed in Silverman 1971), we can see both the assertion of one's ancestors having taken control in the past, and the assertion of autochthony being used as warrants for relations in the present which involve unequal rights and surplus. Banaban explanations of why certain groups have rights to supervise the external windfalls and games often focus on the question of original occupation or subsequent occupation. The interpretation of this situation for Banaba is difficult because of the uneven historical record available to outsiders, and because of its politically contentious nature.

62. This situation may correspond to the "proverbial" statement that women can divide brothers from one another; see discussion in Silverman 1971.

63. Grimble writes, translating from Gilbertese: 'with its brother, the hook.' The Gilbertese term glossed as 'brother' is probably *tarina* 'its same gender sibling, its sibling'.

64. Maude Papers. I assume from Grimble's material on the Gilbertese side that there was a separation of menstruating women from one another; but on this issue in general, see Köngäs-Maranda 1974.

65. At least from a male perspective.

66. Matters of this sort are addressed in the Melanesian ethnography, e.g., Buchbinder and Rappaport 1976, Hogbin 1970, Meggitt 1964. It is interesting to observe that the last-born child in Gilbertese may be referred to, in jest or insult, by a term *(te bukinikoro)* used for a pandanus tree which grows from a discarded pandanus fruit which has already been sucked of its sweet and refreshing goodness by a person. Another word *(te beti)* used for the sucked-out fruit also means 'placenta'. Combined with the data on pre-marital virginity, this mildly suggests a notion that procreative capacity was progressively weakened as used, which might have been linked to the general downward slide of seniority from the elder to the younger members of a sibling set: the elders would have been 'stronger' if they were regarded as the product of their parents' stronger procreative capacity. At the same time, among the Banabans, the last-born child may have had a certain preciousness (cf. Kirsch 1973, on the eldest son and the youngest son), perhaps as the parents' comfort in their old age and as the least competitive for their position. If the strength of procreative capacity was believed to decline with use, there may have been an interesting difference in the use of "procreative" and of "material" capacity. This interpretation, however, is difficult to reconcile with the data on possible sexual relations between people and spouse's same gender siblings. The interpretation could shed an interesting light on the problem of the menstrual taboo, as women would have been involved

not only in unproductive losses, but also in frequent and weakening losses.

67. As far as we know, these people did not make the kind of intense associations between women, death, marriage and sex which have been reported for some peoples in Melanesia. Yet there is an interesting Edenic Banaban narrative inter-relating the origin of sexuality, the origin of death, incest, the younger not listening to the elder and the seductiveness of women, through a tree associated with men (and perhaps genderless) which eternally recreated food, and a female tree which was the tree of creating things. There is a version in Grimble 1923 from Nei Tearia of Banaba. The version differs from that later published by Grimble (1952:63-66) from the same source. Grimble's notes raise certain difficulties in evaluating the published texts (Grimble Papers).

68. During my brief period of linguistic field-work conducted while this manuscript was in press, a Banaban friend alluded to a root crop cultivated on Banaba, which may have been used in some ways similar to swamp taro in the Gilberts. This is my only report of such a crop. Circumstances did not permit me to follow up on this lead.

# REFERENCES

Althusser, Louis
    1969   "Contradiction and overdetermination" and "On the materialist dialectic." In *For Marx*, by L. Althusser. New York: Random House (Vintage).
    1971   "Ideology and ideological state apparatuses." In *Lenin and Philosophy*, by L. Althusser. New York: Monthly Review Press.

Althusser, Louis, and Etienne Balibar
    1970   *Reading Capital.* London: New Left Books.

Balibar, Etienne
    1970   "The basic concepts of historical materialism." In *Reading Capital*, by L. Althusser and E. Balibar. London: New Left Books.

Baran, Paul A., and Paul M. Sweezy
    1968   *Monopoly Capital.* New York: Modern Reader Paperbacks.

Barnett, M.R.
    1975   "A theoretical perspective on racial public policy." In *Blacks in Public Policy*, edited by M.R. Barnett and J.A. Heffner. Pt. Washington, N.Y.: Alfred Press.

Barnett, Stephen A.
    1976   "Approaches to changes in caste ideology in South India." In *Essays on South India*, edited by Burton Stein. Asian Studies Program, Asian Studies at Hawaii, No. 15. Honolulu: University Press of Hawaii.
    1977   *From Structure to Substance: The Past Fifty Years of a South Indian Caste.* Forthcoming.

Bateson, Gregory
    1972   *Steps to an Ecology of Mind.* New York: Ballantine.

Baudrillard, Jean
    1972   *Pour Une Critique de l'Économie Politique de Signe.* Paris: Gallimard.
    1975   *The Mirror of Production.* St. Louis: Telos Press.

Becker, Ernest
    1971   *The Lost Science of Man.* New York: G. Braziller.

Bellah, Robert
 1964  "Religious evolution." *American Sociological Review*
       29:358-374.
Bendix, Reinhard
 1962  *Max Weber: An Intellectual Portrait*. Garden City, N.Y.:
       Doubleday.
Bernstein, Basil
 1972  "A sociolinguistic approach to socialization." In *Direc-
       tions in Sociolinguistics: The Ethnography of Communi-
       cation*, edited by J.J. Gumperz and D. Hymes. New
       York: Holt, Rinehart and Winston.
Bingham, Rev. Hiram
 1953  [1908] *A Gilbertese-English Dictionary*. Boston: Ameri-
       can Board of Commissioners for Foreign Missions.
Buchbinder, Georgeda, and Roy A. Rappaport
 1976  "Fertility and death among the Maring." In *Man and
       Woman in the New Guinea Highlands*, edited by P.
       Brown and G. Buchbinder. American Anthropological
       Association Special Publication No. 8.
Burridge, K.O.L.
 1958  "Marriage in Tangu." *Oceania* 29:44-61.
 1969  *New Heaven, New Earth*. Oxford: Basil Blackwell.
Burrow, J.W.
 1966  *Evolution and Society*. Cambridge: Cambridge Univer-
       sity Press.
Carver, Terrell, ed.
 1975  *Karl Marx: Texts on Method*. Oxford: Basil Blackwell.
Catala, René
 1957  *Report on the Gilbert Islands: Some Aspects of Human
       Ecology*. Atoll Research Bulletin 59. Washington, D.C.:
       Pacific Science Board, National Academy of Sciences,
       National Research Council.
Clement, Wallace
 1975  *The Canadian Corporate Elite*. Toronto: McClelland and
       Stewart.
Cohen, Jere, Lawrence E. Hazelrigg, and Whitney Pope
 1975  "De-Parsonizing Weber." *American Sociological Review*
       40:229-241.

Cornforth, Maurice C.
1952- 1954 *Dialectical Materialism: An Introductory Course.*
3 vols. London: Lawrence and Wishart.

Dalton, George
1965 "Primitive, archaic, and modern economies: Karl Polanyi's contribution to economic anthropology and comparative economy." In *Essays in Economic Anthropology*, edited by P. Bohannon and M. Sahlins. Proceedings of the 1965 Annual Spring Meeting, American Ethnological Society (edited by J. Helm). Seattle: University of Washington Press.

Damon, Fred
1978 "Production and the Circulation of Value on the Other Side of the Kula Ring." Ph.D. dissertation, Princeton University.

Dolgin, Janet
1977 *Jewish Identity and the JDL.* Princeton, N.J.: Princeton University Press.

Douglas, Mary
1966 *Purity and Danger.* New York: Praeger.
1970 *Natural Symbols.* London: Barrie and Rockliff.

Dumont, Louis
1961 "Caste, racism and 'stratification'." *Contributions to Indian Sociology* 5:20-43.
1965 "The modern conception of the individual." *Contributions to Indian Sociology* 8:7-69.
1970 *Homo Hierarchicus.* Chicago: University of Chicago Press.
1971 "Religion, society and politics in the individualistic universe." In *Proceedings of the Royal Anthropological Institute for 1970*:31-41.

Durkheim, Émile
1933 [1902] *The Division of Labor in Society.* Glencoe, Ill.: Free Press.

Eastman, Rev. George
1948 *An English-Gilbertese Vocabulary.* Rongorongo, Beru, Gilbert Islands: London Mission Press.

Edwards, Richard C., Michael Reich, and Thomas E. Weisskopf
1972 *The Capitalist System.* Englewood Cliffs, N.J.: Prentice-

Hall.

Eichler, Margrit
1973    "Women as personal dependents." In *Women in Canada,*
        edited by Marylee Stephenson. Toronto: New Press.

Engels, Frederick
1970    [1884] "The Origin of the Family, Private Property and
        the State." In *Selected Works,* by K. Marx and F. Engels.
        Moscow: Progress Publishers.

Ewen, Stuart
1976    *Captains of Consciousness.* New York: McGraw-Hill.

Firth, R., J. Hubert, and A. Forge
1969    *Families and Their Relatives.* London: Routledge and
        Kegan Paul.

Foucault, Michel
1973    [1966] *The Order of Things.* New York: Random
        House (Vintage).

Frankfurt Institute for Social Research
1973    *Aspects of Sociology.* London: Heinemann Educational.

Friedl, Ernestine
1975    *Women and Men.* New York: Holt, Rinehart and
        Winston.

Geddes, W.H.
1975    *North Tabiteuea Report.* Victoria University of Welling-
        ton, Rural Socio-Economic Survey of the Gilbert and
        Ellice Islands. Wellington: Victoria University of
        Wellington.

Godelier, Maurice
1972    *Rationality and Irrationality in Economics.* London:
        New Left Books.
1974    "Anthropology and biology." *International Social
        Science Journal* 26:611-635.
1977    *Perspectives in Marxist Anthropology.* Cambridge:
        Cambridge University Press.

Goldman, Irving
1970    *Ancient Polynesian Society.* Chicago: University of
        Chicago Press.

Goldmann, Lucien
1973    *The Philosophy of the Enlightenment.* Cambridge,
        Mass.: M.I.T. Press.

1973- 1974 "Introduction to the problems of a sociology of the novel." *Telos* 18:122-135.

1977 *Lukács and Heidegger: Towards a New Philosophy.* London: Routledge and Kegan Paul.

Goodale, Jane C., and Ann Chowning

1971 "The contaminating woman." Paper read at 1971 Annual Meetings, American Anthropological Association.

Grant, George

1970 [1965] *Lament for a Nation: The Defeat of Canadian Nationalism.* Toronto: McClelland and Stewart.

Grimble, Sir Arthur

1921 "From birth to death in the Gilbert Islands." *Journal of the Royal Anthropological Institute* 51:25-54.

1923 "Myths from the Gilbert Islands, II." *Folk-Lore* 34: 370-374.

1933- 1934 *The Migrations of a Pandanus People.* Polynesian Society Memoir No. 12. Wellington: Polynesian Society.

1952 *We Chose The Islands.* New York: Morrow.

1957 *Return to the Islands.* New York: Morrow.

Habermas, Jürgen

1975 *Legitimation Crisis.* Boston: Beacon Press.

Hogbin, Ian

1970 *The Island of Menstruating Men.* Scranton: Chandler.

Hooper, Antony

1976 " 'Eating blood': Tahitian concepts of incest." *Journal of the Polynesian Society* 85:227-241.

Hsu, Francis L.K.

1972 "American core values and national character." In *Psychological Anthropology,* edited by F.L.K. Hsu. New edition. Cambridge, Mass.: Schenkman.

Hymes, Dell, ed.

1972 *Reinventing Anthropology.* New York: Pantheon.

Jarvie, I.C.

1975 "Epistle to the anthropologists." *American Anthropologist* 77:253-266.

Jensen, Phyllis

MS. "The name of the relationship is called 'love'." Anthropology paper, University of Western Ontario, 1975.

Kirsch, A. Thomas
    1973    *Feasting and Social Oscillation: A Working Paper on
            Religion and Society in Upland Southeast Asia.* Cornell
            University, Southeast Asia Program, Data Paper No. 92.
            Ithaca, N.Y.: Southeast Asia Program, Department of
            Asian Studies, Cornell University.
Koch, Gerd
    1965    *Materielle Kultur der Gilbert-Inseln.* Berlin: Museum fur
            Volkerkunde.
Köngäs-Maranda, Elli
    1974    "Lau, Malaita: 'A woman is an alien spirit'." In *Many
            Sisters,* edited by C. Matthiasson. New York: Free
            Press.
Kuhn, Thomas S.
    1970    *The Structure of Scientific Revolutions.* Second edition.
            Chicago: University of Chicago Press.
Labby, David
    1976a   *The Demystification of Yap.* Chicago: University of
            Chicago Press.
    1976b   "Incest as cannibalism: The Yapese analysis." *Journal of
            the Polynesian Society* 85:171-179.
Lakatos, Imre, and Alan Musgrave, eds.
    1970    *Criticism and the Growth of Knowledge.* Cambridge:
            University Press.
Lambert, Bernd
    1963    "Rank and Ramage in the Northern Gilbert Islands."
            Ph.D. dissertation, University of California, Berkeley.
    1966    "The economic activities of a Gilbertese chief." In
            *Political Anthropology,* edited by M.J. Swartz, V.W.
            Turner and A. Tuden. Chicago: Aldine.
    1970    "Adoption, guardianship, and social stratification in the
            Northern Gilbert Islands." In *Adoption in Eastern
            Oceania,* edited by Vern Carroll. Honolulu: University
            of Hawaii Press.
    1971    "The Gilbert Islands: Micro-Individualism." In *Land
            Tenure in the Pacific,* edited by Ron Crocombe. Mel-
            bourne: Oxford University Press.
Lane, Robert E.
    1962    *Political Ideology.* New York: Free Press of Glencoe.

Leach, Edmund R.
  1961  *Rethinking Anthropology.* London: University of London, Athlone Press.
Lee, Dorothy D.
  1959  [1950] "Codifications of reality: Lineal and nonlineal." In *Freedom and Culture,* by Dorothy D. Lee. Englewood Cliffs, N.J.: Prentice-Hall (Spectrum).
Lefebvre, Henri
  1971  *Everyday Life in the Modern World.* New York: Harper and Row (Harper Torchbooks).
Lévi-Strauss, Claude
  1963  "Social structure." In *Structural Anthropology,* by C. Lévi-Strauss. Garden City, N.Y.: Basic Books.
  1966  *The Savage Mind.* London: Weidenfeld and Nicolson.
  1969  [1949] *The Elementary Structures of Kinship.* London: Eyre and Spottiswoode.
Locke, John
  1965  [1698] *Two Treatises of Government.* New York: New American Library (Mentor).
Lukács, Georg
  1971  [1922] "Reification and the consciousness of the proletariat." In *History and Class Consciousness,* by G. Lukács. Cambridge, Mass.: M.I.T. Press.
Lundberg, F.
  1968  *The Rich and the Super-Rich.* New York: L. Stuart.
Lundsgaarde, Henry P.
  1966  "Cultural Adaptation in the Southern Gilbert Islands." Ph.D. dissertation, University of Wisconsin, Madison.
  1970  "Some legal aspects of Gilbertese adoption." In *Adoption in Eastern Oceania,* edited by Vern Carroll. Honolulu: University of Hawaii Press.
  1974  "The evolution of tenure principles on Tamana Island, Gilbert Islands." In *Land Tenure in Oceania,* edited by H.P. Lundsgaarde. Honolulu: University Press of Hawaii.
Lundsgaarde, Henry P., and Martin G. Silverman
  1972  "Category and group in Gilbertese kinship." *Ethnology* 11:95-110.
Luomala, Katherine
  1965  "Humorous narratives about individual resistance to

food-distribution customs in Tabiteuea, Gilbert Islands." *Journal of American Folklore* 78:28-45.

1974    "The *Cyrtosperma* systemic pattern: Aspects of production in the Gilbert Islands." *Journal of the Polynesian Society* 83:14-34.

Macpherson, C.B.

1964    *The Political Theory of Possessive Individualism.* London: Oxford University Press.

Maddock, Kenneth

1972    *The Australian Aborigines.* London: Allen Lane, The Penguin Press.

Magdoff, JoAnn, and Janet Dolgin

1977    "The ethnic medium." In *Yearbook of Symbolic Anthropology,* edited by E. Schwimmer. In press.

Maine, Sir Henry Sumner

1970    [1884] *Ancient Law.* Reprint of Tenth Edition. Gloucester, Mass.: Peter Smith.

Mandel, Ernest

1970    *Marxist Economic Theory,* volume 1. New York: Monthly Review Press.

Manuel, George, and Michael Posluns

1974    *The Fourth World.* Don Mills, Ont.: Collier Macmillan Canada Ltd.

Marchak, M. Patricia

1975    *Ideological Perspectives on Canada.* Toronto: McGraw-Hill Ryerson.

Marx, Karl

1964    [1844] *The Economic and Philosophical Manuscripts of 1844.* New York: International Publishers.

1967    [1867] *Capital,* volume 1. New York: International Publishers.

1967    [1894] *Capital,* volume 3. New York: International Publishers.

1970    [1852] "The Eighteenth Brumaire of Louis Bonaparte." In *Selected Works,* by K. Marx and F. Engels. Moscow: Progress Publishers.

1973    [1857-1858] *Grundrisse.* Translated with a Foreword by Martin Nicolaus. Harmondsworth: Penguin.

Marx, Karl, and Frederick Engels
1970a [1846] *The German Ideology.* New York: International Publishers.
1970b [1848] "Manifesto of the Communist Party." In *Selected Works,* by K. Marx and F. Engels. Moscow: Progress Publishers.

Maude, H.C., and H.E. Maude
1932 "The social organization of Banaba or Ocean Island, Central Pacific." *Journal of the Polynesian Society* 41:262-301.

Maude, H.E.
1963 *The Evolution of the Gilbertese Boti.* Polynesian Society Memoir No. 35. Wellington: Polynesian Society.

Mauss, Marcel
1938 "Une categorie de l'esprit humain: la notion de personne, celle de 'moi'." *Journal of the Royal Anthropological Institute* 68:263-281.
1970 [1925] *The Gift.* London: Routledge and Kegan Paul.

Meggitt, M.J.
1964 "Male-female relationships in the Highlands of Australian New Guinea." In *New Guinea: The Central Highlands,* edited by J. Watson. *American Anthropologist* 66(4), Part 2:204-224.

Meillassoux, Claude
1972 "From reproduction to production." *Economy and Society* 1:93-105.

Meissner, M., E. Humphreys, S. Meis, and W. Scheu
1975 "No exit for wives." *Canadian Review of Sociology and Anthropology* 12:424-439.

Murdock, George P.
1972 "Anthropology's mythology." In *Proceedings of the Royal Anthropological Institute for 1971:17-24.*

Murphy, Robert F.
1971 *The Dialectics of Social Life.* New York: Basic Books.

Needham, Rodney
1971a "Introduction." In *Rethinking Kinship and Marriage,* edited by R. Needham. Association of Social Anthropologists, Monographs 11. London: Tavistock.
1971b "Remarks on the analysis of kinship and marriage." In

*Rethinking Kinship and Marriage,* edited by R. Needham. Association of Social Anthropologists, Monographs 11. London: Tavistock.

Nikitin, P.
1966    *Fundamentals of Political Economy.* Moscow: Progress Publishers.

Ollman, Bertell
1971    *Alienation.* Cambridge: University Press.

Parkin, Frank
1971    *Class Inequality and Political Order.* London: MacGibbon and Kee.

Parsons, Talcott
1951    *The Social System.* Glencoe, Ill.: Free Press.
1966    *Societies.* Englewood Cliffs, N.J.: Prentice-Hall.

Piaget, Jean
1950    *Introduction à l'Épistemologie Génétique.* Paris: Presses Universitaires de France.

Polanyi, Karl
1944    *The Great Transformation.* New York, Toronto: Farrar and Rinehart.

Poulantzas, Nicos
1973    *Political Power and Social Classes.* London: NLB, Sheed and Ward.
1974    "Internationalization of capitalist relations and the nation-state." *Economy and Society* 3:145-179.

Rappaport, Roy A.
1967    *Pigs for the Ancestors.* New Haven: Yale University Press.

Rivière, P.G.
1971    "Marriage: A reassessment." In *Rethinking Kinship and Marriage,* edited by R. Needham. Association of Social Anthropologists, Monographs 11. London: Tavistock.

Rowbotham, Sheila
1973    *Woman's Consciousness, Man's World.* Harmondsworth: Penguin.

Sabatier, Revérénd Père Ernest
1954    *Dictionnaire Gilbertin-Français.* Tabuiroa, Gilbert Islands: Sacred Heart Mission.

Sahlins, Marshall
   1958   *Social Stratification in Polynesia.* Publications of the
          American Ethnological Society. Seattle: University of
          Washington Press.
   1972   *Stone Age Economics.* Chicago: Aldine.
Salisbury, Richard
   1962   *From Stone to Steel.* Melbourne: Melbourne University
          Press.
Sartre, Jean-Paul
   1965   *Anti-Semite and Jew.* New York: Schocken.
Scheffler, H.W., and F.G. Lounsbury
   1971   *A Study in Structural Semantics.* Englewood Cliffs,
          N.J.: Prentice-Hall.
Schieffelin, Edward L.
   1976   *The Sorrow of the Lonely and the Burning of the
          Dancers.* New York: St. Martin's Press.
Schneider, David M.
   1968   *American Kinship.* Englewood Cliffs, N.J.: Prentice-
          Hall.
   1970   "Kinship, nationality and religion in American culture."
          In *Forms of Symbolic Action,* edited by R. Spencer.
          Proceedings of the 1969 Annual Spring Meeting, Ameri-
          can Ethnological Society.
   1972   "What is kinship all about?" In *Kinship Studies in the
          Morgan Centennial Year,* edited by P. Reining. Washing-
          ton D.C.: Anthropological Society of Washington.
Schneider, Harold
   1974   *Economic Man.* New York: Free Press.
Sebag, Lucien
   1964   *Marxisme et Structuralisme.* Paris: Payot.
Silverman, Martin G.
   1970   "Banaban adoption." In *Adoption in Eastern Oceania,*
          edited by Vern Carroll. Honolulu: University of Hawaii
          Press.
   1971   *Disconcerting Issue: Meaning and Struggle in a Resettled
          Pacific Community.* Chicago: University of Chicago
          Press.
   1972   "Ambiguation and disambiguation in field work and
          analysis." In *Crossing Cultural Boundaries,* edited by

S.T. Kimball and J.B. Watson. San Francisco: Chandler.

1977    "Making sense: A study of a Banaban meeting." In *Exiles and Migrants in Oceania*, edited by M.D. Lieber. Honolulu: University Press of Hawaii.

1978a   "Some problems in the understanding of Oceanic kinship." In *The Changing Pacific*, edited by N. Gunson. Melbourne: Oxford University Press.

1978b   "Locating 'possession' and 'objectification' in Gilbertese." *Proceedings of the 1977 Congress*. Canadian Ethnology Society. In press.

Smith, Dorothy E.

1973    "Women, the family and corporate capitalism." In *Women in Canada*, edited by Marylee Stephenson. Toronto: New Press.

Steiner, Franz

1967    [1956] *Taboo*. Harmondsworth. Penguin.

Stevenson, Robert Louis

1905    *In the South Seas. The Biographical Edition of Stevenson's Works*. New York: Scribner's.

Stocking, George W.

1974    "Introduction: The basic assumptions of Boasian anthropology." In *The Shaping of American Anthropology, 1883-1911: A Franz Boas Reader*. New York: Basic Books.

Strathern, Marilyn

1972    *Women in Between*. London: Seminar Press.

MS.     "The achievement of sex: Paradoxes in Hagen gender-thinking." *Yearbook of Symbolic Anthropology*. In press.

Swartz, M.J., V.W. Turner, and A.Tuden

1966    "Introduction." In *Political Anthropology*, edited by M.J. Swartz, V.W. Turner and A. Tuden. Chicago: Aldine.

Terray, Emmanuel

1972    "Historical materialism and segmentary lineage-based societies." In *Marxism and "Primitive" Societies*, by E. Terray. New York: Monthly Review Press.

Trudeau, Pierre Elliott

1974    [1956] In *The Asbestos Strike*, edited by Pierre E.

Trudeau. Toronto: James Lewis and Samuel.

Tyler, Stephen A., ed.
1969 *Cognitive Anthropology.* New York: Holt, Rinehart and Winston.

Wagner, Roy
1975 *The Invention of Culture.* Englewood Cliffs, N.J.: Prentice-Hall.

Weber, Max
1964 [1947] *The Theory of Social and Economic Organization.* Translated by A.M. Henderson and Talcott Parsons. Edited with an introduction by Talcott Parsons. New York: Free Press of Glencoe.
1968 *Economy and Society,* volume 1. Translated by E. Fiscoff et al. Edited by G. Roth and C. Wittich. New York: Bedminster Press.

Webster, J.
1866 *The Last Cruise of the Wanderer.* Sydney: Cunninghame.

Weiner, Annette B.
1976 *Women of Value, Men of Renown: New Perspectives on Trobriand Exchange.* Austin: University of Texas Press.

Whorf, Benjamin L.
1956 [1941] "The relation of habitual thought and behavior to language." In *Language, Thought, and Reality,* by B.L. Whorf. Edited by John Carroll. Cambridge, Mass.: Technology Press of M.I.T.

Williams, Raymond
1973 "Base and superstructure in Marxist cultural theory." *New Left Review* 82:3-16.

Wolff, Kurt H., ed.
1964 [1950] *The Sociology of Georg Simmel.* New York: Free Press of Glencoe.